ENDORSEMENT

"The artist Georgia O'Keefe once remarked, 'Nobody sees a flower, really. It is so small. We haven't time, and to see takes time.' So too, the living God who is ever-present yet invisible to the eye is often missed, overlooked, or thought to be not there at all. But for those who take the time to train the mystic eye, God can not only be seen, but praised and celebrated as well.

"Christine Fisher is one who not only sees God all around her, but in her first book, *God's Presence Illuminated*, has shared those glimpses of God with us as well, that we too might discover His presence in our lives. Christine's second book, *God's Love Illuminated*, is based on the Christian truth that God is love, and where there is love, there God is found. Though the word 'love' is used in a variety of ways in today's culture, true love – that which flows from God and is God – is brought to our attention in this book, so that we too might discern the love of God that exists all around us."

Fr. Michael P. Galuppi
Syracuse, NY

Other books by Christine M. Fisher:

God's Presence Illuminated: Treasured Thoughts to Inspire Hope and Light

GOD'S LOVE
Illuminated

A 90-DAY DEVOTIONAL

Treasured Thoughts to Inspire Walking in God's Abundant Love

CHRISTINE M. FISHER

God's Love Illuminated
Treasured Thoughts to Inspire Walking in God's Abundant Love
Christine M. Fisher

To contact the author:
christine@hopetoinspireyou.com
www.hopetoinspireyou.com

Published by

Mary Ethel

Mary Ethel Eckard
Frisco, Texas

ISBN (Print): 978-1-7357853-6-3
ISBN (E-book): 978-1-7357853-7-0

CONTENTS

SECTION 2: GOD'S LOVE ILLUMINATED IN SCRIPTURE... 55

SECTION 3: GOD'S LOVE ILLUMINATED IN ORDINARY LIFE 133

SECTION 4: GOD'S LOVE ILLUMINATED IN MINISTRY.... 189

DEDICATION

This book is written with thanksgiving to God for His great love in sending Jesus as an atoning sacrifice for our sins. Jesus' love has given us the victory in our lives.

I dedicate this work, with love, to all those who have supported my writing ministry since 2014. That's when I began expressing my heart and love for the Lord through my weekly thoughts at www.hopetoinspireyou.com. My life has been enriched through meeting many people while sharing my first book, *God's Presence Illuminated*, published in 2020.

"I'm a little pencil in the hand of a writing God, who is sending a love letter to the world." –Mother Teresa

God is always writing and sending His love letter to us through the encounters we have. He sends us love letters all through our days.

May you experience God's love illuminated in your heart and life through this little pencil.

FOREWORD

It's not often I get to know a published writer. Getting to know Christine has been a real joy. I first met her as a member of St. Ambrose parish, and then as time went by, I became an avid reader of her blog. When we met several years ago, I discovered that she has a wonderful, spiritual side that was becoming more and more open to the idea of sharing with her friends and family.

Christine weaves together a practical spirituality in which she has allowed her heart to be filled with her daily experiences of God and an intellectual spirituality that has grown out of years of reading Scripture and praying to Christ in His presence in the Christian Church.

As a Franciscan, I marvel at Christine's ability to easily find God in nature, which she has expressed in words and pictures. I highly recommend to anyone searching for their own spiritual journey to let Christine's words and thoughts flow over them so they can share the feeling of God's love.

Deacon Thomas M. Harley
Endicott, NY

PREFACE

After writing my first book, *God's Presence Illuminated,* someone asked me how I am able to recognize God's hand in the smallest of things. In hindsight, I can confidently answer the question by sharing a little of my testimony. They say those who have had the scare of death are blessed with eyes that have been opened to the simplicities and greater purpose and callings of life. I fit into that category.

In March 2013, I received a diagnosis of breast cancer. It was an unwelcome interruption and it felt like my world fell apart. My life changed in the blink of an eye. My faith that I thought was strong seemed to crumble with hearing those words.

I was very fortunate my cancer was not invasive, as it was caught early. After a few procedures and surgeries, my greatest struggle was in deciding the subsequent treatment options. I am not one to go against medical protocol. I struggled to hear God's voice and agonized over the course of action that was best for me. Eventually, I found myself having peace in opting against the recommended radiation treatment.

To date, God has given me eight years of a clean bill of health with no recurrence of cancer. But that doesn't mean my life trajectory was not altered by the cancer scare! Walking through this sparked a closer relationship with God and helped me love others more. I came to a new awareness of the value and gift of life.

Wanting to step more into life and ministry and desiring to follow my favorite band, Third Day, I joined social media in early 2014. I came across a man who wrote daily blogs about the simple things in life and ended each writing with scripture. His thoughts touched my heart and I wanted to share God in that same way. So, in September 2014, I built a website, www.hopetoinspireyou.com, and wrote my first weekly blog with the intent of sharing God in the ordinary. The more God-sightings I wrote about, the more my heart, eyes, and ears were opened to see and experience God in the ordinary. The more I dug into scripture to learn about God's love and the life of Jesus, the more I began to see the needs of others and desired to reach out and share the Lord.

Though I walked in faith before the cancer diagnosis, my faith journey has grown so much. God used that time in my life to show me His love and His goodness. Writing helps me process the things God shows me, and my hope and desire is to help others see God in a new way – in the ordinary things of life.

INTRODUCTION

"…God is love…"
~ 1 John 4:16

My Pastor has mentioned several times this simple yet powerful sentence. These three words have such a powerful impact in our lives. *God is love!* His love is everywhere.

"'Teacher, which is the greatest commandment in the Law?' Jesus replied:
'Love the Lord your God with all your heart and with all your soul
and with all your mind. This is the first and greatest commandment.
And the second is like it: Love your neighbor as yourself.'"
~ Matthew 22:36-39

I became more aware of God's love beginning in mid-December 2020. It was the day I looked up in the sky and was greeted by a pink heart shaped cloud while walking and praying. I was in awe of its beauty. I was reminded of a walk earlier in the year with a friend who often sees heart clouds around the time of the anniversary of a loved one's death. The hearts remind her of God's love.

The next day as I was walking, I saw a wet heart shape on the curb. Since then, no matter the season, God daily puts heart shape reminders in my path. They might be in the form of clouds, stones, flower pedals, raindrops, or even spilled water on my counter.

These heart reminders make God's love more real for me. I know He is working to soften my heart, transforming it from a heart of stone to a heart of flesh. I sense I am growing in realizing the unconditional love God has for me. He makes me smile when I see these hearts and I am in awe of His goodness. In turn, His love is helping me grow in unconditional love for myself and in extending it to others.

God is love. He lives in us, so His love is in us too. God's love is evident in the people we interact with daily, the Scriptures, the ordinary of daily life, and in the ministry we do in His name.

My prayer is that these thoughts will encourage you to see God's love through a different lens or to walk closer in God's love. As you take time to reflect on each story, may you be inspired to embrace God's abundant love in your faith journey. May the closing scripture for each day reveal a facet of God's love for you personally.

God's love illuminated.

Section 1

GOD'S LOVE ILLUMINATED IN PEOPLE

"A new command I give you: Love one another.
As I have loved you, so you must love one another."
~ John 13:34

Jesus gave us an extraordinary example of loving others. He embodied love and compassion even for the worst of sinners. He saw goodness in everyone because He knew they, too, were made in God's image.

Jesus shared this command to love one another as He modeled love to His disciples. Right after giving this command, He predicted that Peter would disown knowing Him three times before the rooster crowed. Jesus loved Peter despite his denial, and He built His church upon the faith of Peter and the other disciples. The Greek word for Peter means rock. In Matthew 16:18, Jesus said, *"You are Peter, and on this rock I will build my church."* God used the faith of Peter and the other disciples as the foundation of the church, a faith evidenced by their love for God and for others.

We, being disciples of Jesus, are given this same command to love one another with the agape love Jesus shows us.

God's love illuminated in people.

1

You are Beautiful

You are beautiful.
Yes, that means you, the one reading these words.
You are beautiful.
Let those words sink into your heart and mind.

Do you know who thinks you are most beautiful? God, your Father, the One who thought of you, created you, and formed you in your mother's womb. His view of you is the only one that matters.

You are alive to fulfill His design for you.

I am fascinated by the ripple effect our actions and choices have. I see God at work in everything. There is such meaning in how everything is connected and intertwined.

One Christmas season, my friend posted a picture showing how he was spreading kindness. He made care packages to distribute to the homeless people in his community. It inspired me to do something similar.

The next week as I was preparing to serve at our local soup kitchen, I wanted to give the guests a little Christmas gift to take home. I stopped at a store and headed down an aisle to browse for items I could include in the gift packages.

Suddenly a gentleman appeared. He said, "May I ask you a question?" I responded, "Yes." (I thought he was going to ask for money.) He asked, "Are you married?" I quickly answered, "Yes," to which he replied, "You are beautiful. He is a lucky guy."

As I was relaying the story to a friend, I said, "Maybe he was trying to do an act of kindness, or maybe he was doing it on a dare." My friend replied, "Oh my goodness, that's awesome. He only pointed out what everyone else sees. You are beautiful!" And then, "Maybe he was a messenger from God, an angel! You never know!"

Her response struck me and made me think. Yes, maybe the gentleman was an angel in disguise. Maybe it was a message from God. A message we all need to be reminded of.

You are beautiful!
Beautiful because God created you.
Beautiful because God lives in you.
Beautiful because you are created in God's image and likeness.
Beautiful because God loves you with an everlasting love.
Beautiful because God sent Jesus to die for your sins.
Beautiful because God calls you His child.

"See what great love the Father has lavished on us, that we should be called children of God! And that is what we are! The reason the world does not know us is that it did not know him."
~ 1 John 3:1

Christine M. Fisher

2

Impacting Others

Do you ever think your life doesn't have an impact on others?
Do you ever think your life is unimportant?
Do you ever think since you are just a simple, ordinary
person, your life does not leave an imprint on others?

We need to be available to listen to, empathize with, and share compassion and God's love with others. The struggle is, we often do not let others know what we are thinking or feeling. We often put up walls that prevent us from sharing our true selves.

NO MAN IS AN ISLAND

Have you ever felt…

> you were trying to open up to someone who listened with their ears and not their heart?
> someone didn't respond when you needed them most?
> a friend was too wrapped up in their own issues to help?
> jealous of a friend, thinking they had it all together, so you put up an emotional wall?
> you only get hurt if you try to share?
> people don't really care?

Keep in mind: God is a triune God, Father, Son, and Spirit forming a community. Being created in God's image, we, too, are a community. We have brothers and sisters in faith all over the world. We need to be available for others and let them know we are for them, not against them.

FRIENDS COME AND GO LIKE THE WAVES OF THE OCEAN, BUT TRUE FRIENDS STICK LIKE AN OCTOPUS ON YOUR FACE!

I am more like an octopus with my friends. I might not know or interact with lots of people, but the ones I do, I consider friends. I do not want to see them leave like the waves of the ocean. Once a friend, always a friend.

How can you be a true friend to others?
Do you have some octopus friends?

"IF YOU DON'T IMPACT PEOPLE, THEN THIS WHOLE THING WAS A WASTE." –Chris Rosati

Chris Rosati was a man who lost his battle with ALS after six years. After his diagnosis, he decided to face his fear of the life-ending disease by thinking of others by doing random acts of kindness. He began handing out donuts to passersby on the street and included an inspiring message. This action sparked a ripple effect of people doing good deeds.

I like this definition of impact: "To have a strong effect on someone or something."

Who has had the greatest impact on your life?
Whose life have you impacted?

Each of our lives are important and vital to others. We are each a link, a stepping-stone in others' lives. We are puzzle pieces. Your life impacts those around you. You are a stepping-stone to help others reach their potential. You are a vital puzzle piece in others' lives.

Christine M. Fisher

Reach out to someone who has influenced your life and let them know you appreciate them. It is important to share how they have made your life better. You never know when it will be your last breath.

"But since you excel in everything—in faith, in speech, in knowledge, in complete earnestness and in the love we have kindled in you—see that you also excel in this grace of giving."
~ 2 Corinthians 8:7

3

God's Little Ones

I enjoy holding infants and little ones. They seem to enjoy me too. There is something about loving children that makes me feel closer to God.

Last year I was honored to hold a little boy with blonde hair and blue eyes. His foster parents were watching their older son play baseball, and I wanted to give them a break so they could concentrate on the game. My best "holding" times are when the babies snuggle, comfortable and cozy, and fall asleep on my chest. I like the feeling of their peaceful breathing.

This year the same family has a little foster girl who looks like an angel. She has beautiful, squeezable cheeks and perfect lips. Her dark, curly hair and big brown eyes melt my heart. Her peaceful demeanor adds to her angelic aura.

As I interact with these beautiful little ones, I think how special the people who foster or adopt these children are. What a blessing there are people willing to help the birth parents, who, due to whatever the circumstances, cannot take care of their children. Sometimes what is best is letting someone else care for them. What a difficult decision. We should support them and their decision. Willingness to assist those who care for God's children, young or old, is needed too.

As I see and hold these beautiful babies, I think about how…

> pure and innocent they are.
> they make people smile and love on them.
> angelic and beautiful they are.
> they rely on adults for all their needs.

Christine M. Fisher

soothing it is for them to be given a warm embrace or back rub.

they evoke unconditional love.

they can rest so peacefully wrapped in our arms.

easy it is to love them.

we can see God's reflection in them.

Interacting with children makes me think about how God, our Father, views us. Have you thought about how you are God's adopted son/daughter? What a powerful thought to ponder.

"He predestined us for adoption to himself as sons/daughters through Jesus Christ, according to the purpose of his will."
~ Ephesians 1:5 (ESV)

"The Spirit you received does not make you slaves, so that you live in fear again; rather, the Spirit you received brought about your adoption to sonship/daughtership. And by him we cry, 'Abba, Father.'"
~ Romans 8:15

"But when the fullness of time had come, God sent forth his Son, born of woman, born under the law, to redeem those who were under the law, so that we might receive adoption as sons/daughters. And because you are sons/daughters, God has sent the Spirit of his Son into our hearts, crying, 'Abba! Father!' So you are no longer a slave, but a son/daughter, and if a son/daughter, then an heir through God."
~ Galatians 4:4-7 (ESV)

I believe all these feelings and emotions are also what God experiences when He thinks of us.

Yes, I believe God…

sees how pure and innocent we are.

smiles and loves us infinitely.

sees our angelic and beautiful selves that He created.

wants us to rely on Him for everything.

has His loving arms outstretched to embrace us.

has unconditional love for us no matter what we do.

wants us to rest peacefully in His arms even during the storms of life.

looks at us with great love.

sees His reflection when He looks at us.

Keep in mind how you are God's adopted son/daughter, even made in His image and likeness. God's love for you is everlasting and unconditional.

"I am writing to remind you, dear friends, that we should love one another. This is not a new commandment, but one we have had from the beginning."
~ 2 John 1:5 (NLT)

4

Reflecting Jesus

Soaking up God's beautiful creation near bodies of water is one of my favorite pastimes. One Sunday, my view at the park was a small body of water with a fountain. I found my perfect spot at a picnic table and busied myself with reading. I was surprised when I looked up to see geese in the water.

I watched the geese go into the water for a bit and then walk around the land. They kept repeating the sequence. One goose appeared to be the leader. At one point, they were frolicking and making noise as they played in the water, all going under for a bit and then flapping their wings. I noticed some of their feathers floating along the ripples of water and saw a parallel with our lives.

Imagine the feathers representing a piece of us: A giving of ourselves, our life that influences and touches others. Each interaction we have has a ripple effect on the next person. The more we give, the more we gain, and the more ripples of influence we spread.

It was God's perfect timing for me to hear a sermon that shared this same sentiment. As the preacher pointed out, the ripple effects of our lives are a reflection of Christ in us. The ripples of our lives touch the next person, enriching their life and reflecting Jesus to the world.

The story of the Samaritan woman who Jesus met at the well (John 4:1-42) is an example of the ripple effect our lives can have on others. While conversing with this woman, Jesus revealed Himself as the Messiah. What happened when she realized who she was talking to?

"The woman left her water jar beside the well and ran back to the village, telling everyone, 'Come and see a man who told me everything I ever did! Could he possibly be the Messiah?'"
~ John 4:28-29 (NLT)

"Many Samaritans from the village believed in Jesus because the woman had said, 'He told me everything I ever did!' When they came out to see him, they begged him to stay in their village. So he stayed for two days, long enough for many more to hear his message and believe."
~ John 4:39-41 (NLT)

Jesus touched her life so profoundly that she ran to share the Good News with those in her village. The ripple effect of her life touched many others who also came to believe because of her testimony. Imagine the continued ripple effect of each of those people in spreading the Good News. May Jesus in you reflect to every person you meet, like the feathers from the geese floating along the ripples of the water.

"Father, I want these whom you have given me to be with me where I am. Then they can see all the glory you gave me because you loved me even before the world began!"
~ John 17:24 (NLT)

5

Living Love

I read two books by author, motivational speaker, and lawyer Bob Goff, *Everybody Always* and *Love Does*. These books are filled with engaging stories from Bob's experiences of loving others. He includes his email and phone number in his books because he wants to "live love" and be available to anyone who might be in need.

After reading the books, I wanted to let him know how inspiring his books are. They even make me smile and laugh. I stepped out of my comfort zone and called him. As he states in his books, he does not let his phone go to voice mail. The real Bob Goff answered the phone!

During our brief conversation, I shared with him what I called to say. Out of the blue he said, "You should write a book." I could not believe my ears because, guess what I was doing? I was writing a book! When I told Goff, he said, "Great. People need to hear your words." This was another confirmation for publishing my first book.

Reading Goff's books, I am reminded of the two greatest commandments Jesus gave:

> *"And one of them, a lawyer, asked him a question to test him. 'Teacher, which is the great commandment in the Law?' And he said to him, 'You shall love the Lord your God with all your heart and with all your soul and with all your mind. This is the great and first commandment. And a second is like it: You shall love your neighbor as yourself. On these two commandments depend all the Law and the Prophets.'"*
> ~ Matthew 22:35-40 (ESV)

These verses refer to agape love, which is a benevolent, sacrificial, active, serving love – not a feeling love. Love is a verb in this case.

> Are you truly living love?
> Are you loving God with all your heart, soul, and mind?
> Are you loving your neighbor as yourself?

When I correspond with my co-workers via email, I include a heartfelt greeting to help brighten their day, which helps break down walls. One day I received an email that said, "I always appreciate what you say in your emails. Your choice of words are kind, sweet and nice."

One co-worker emails often with work detail. During the pandemic, we exchanged words of encouragement. Recently, our conversations have expanded to include life's experiences. These stories helped me reflect on fulfilling Jesus' two greatest commandments and living love like Goff shares in his books.

Despite the difficult situations, my co-worker lived love and loved his neighbor by...

> stopping as he saw a tragic event unfold.
> sharing what he witnessed.
> staying with an animal that was dying.
> taking a neighbor, who fell earlier in the day, to the emergency room.
> making sure another neighbor was taken care of.
> assisting a neighbor who had a stroke.
> rescuing and caring for an abandoned dog.
> being available for the neighbor in the emergency room to talk via phone.

I shared with him how I saw God using his compassion and kindness in these events. Because of his love for God, he loved his neighbor.

Reading Goff's books inspires me to live out God's love with everybody, always. We might think because our lives are simple and ordinary, we can't live love. Living love moment-by-moment takes many shapes and forms.

A simple "Have a nice day" can start a ripple effect of love and goodness.
Sharing compassion and kindness is important.
Encouraging someone by letting them know you
are thinking and praying for them.
Sharing Christ can be as simple as holding a door for someone.
Sharing kind words is living love.

Be encouraged to keep living love,
sharing Christ in you with others
in whatever capacity you have.

In living love, you are fulfilling Jesus' greatest commandment.
What a great purpose to live by until the Lord calls you home.

*"I pray that your love will overflow more and more, and that you
will keep on growing in knowledge and understanding."*
~ Philippians 1:9 (NLT)

6

Shine Your Light

Have you ever been burdened, in a room full of people, and felt alone? Nobody seemed to notice you, and nobody seemed to care. Did you need someone to be Christ in the flesh?

Lonely, hurting, and burdened people are all around us. What will you do about it? How can you be Christ for someone who is hurting?

Christ told us we are the light of the world. We are to shine brightly, so all people will see our light. We cannot afford to hide our light, which is so needed in this world.

One way for our light to shine is by being there for one another during the rough times. We should be attentive enough to notice when someone is heavily burdened and care enough to listen with our heart, not just our ears. We may begin to understand their situation from their perspective. It is then God can use us to help them through their problem.

Do you know someone who…

> needs prayer to help them through a difficult situation?
> could use a few dollars to buy food?
> could use a ride to church or the store?
> needs some handiwork done around their house?
> just needs to talk?

What are ways you can shine your light and be Christ to those in need?

Can you...

>pray?
>
>encourage them through a kind word or note?
>
>share your treasure?
>
>share your time?
>
>share your talent?

>*"The King will reply, 'I tell you the truth, whatever you did for one of the least of these brothers and sisters of mine, you did for me.'"*
>~ Matthew 26:40

When the time comes and we meet the Lord face-to-face, I wonder if these are some questions He might ask:

>Did your light shine enough to care about others?
>
>Were you there for them?
>
>How much of Christ in you did you share?
>
>Did you sacrifice your comfort to be Christ for others?

>*"So show them your love, and prove to all the churches that our boasting about you is justified."*
>~ 2 Corinthians 8:24 (NLT)

7

Kindness Matters

You, my friend, are a valuable instrument of God's love. You have the power daily to influence God's kingdom for the better. Do you believe that deep in your heart?

Seeking God in the little things and sharing those things with others is an honor and blesses our own lives at the same time. We do not all have the gift of encouragement, but we can all encourage one another in simple, little ways on this journey of life.

BE THE REASON SOMEONE SMILES TODAY

Can you try making one person smile each day? That is easy enough, right? We can all do that. I bet, if you start consciously thinking about it with one person, you will want to keep the smiles going. It might be contagious.

What are some practical ways you can make someone smile?

Some things that come to mind are...

> giving a genuine compliment about someone's character.
> making eye contact with someone as you say "Hello."
> sending a text or ending your emails with a sincere "Have a great day."
> passing along special Bible verses to brighten a friend's day.
> taking time to check on an elderly or sick neighbor.
> paying for the order of someone behind you in the drive-thru line.
> taking time to listen and understand someone.

KINDNESS MATTERS

In all the actions above, we extend kindness to others. It reminds me of the example of Jesus. He showed love and kindness to those He encountered.

Reach out to others and be a blessing by showing kindness. Even if the kindness is not reciprocated, you can feel good knowing you did your part to bless another and share God's love.

> "Remember, there's no such thing as a small act of kindness. Every act creates a ripple with no logical end." –Scott Adams

"PEOPLE MAY FORGET WHAT YOU SAID OR WHAT YOU DID, BUT NOT HOW YOU MADE THEM FEEL."
–Maya Angelou

Ultimately, kindness is about making people feel special, important, valued, respected, and loved. These are the things that matter. We are all made in God's image. Every day is a new day, a new beginning. Daily strive to make the world a better place for at least one person.

I will leave you to ponder these thoughts:

> "Every time you smile at someone, it is an action of love, a gift to that person, a beautiful thing." –Mother Teresa

> "The smallest acts of kindness can make the biggest differences in someone's life. Do your best and let God do the rest." –Ben Carson

KINDNESS MATTERS

"Therefore, as God's chosen people, holy and dearly loved, clothe yourselves with compassion, kindness, humility, gentleness and patience."
~ Colossians 3:12

8

Faith in Action

Faith in action is something we are called to daily. It is not enough to just know about or hear God's Word. We need to put flesh and blood on that knowledge by taking action. When we have a personal relationship with Christ, we eagerly look for ways we can share His Light. We shine the Light within us by our faith in action.

How can we live out our faith each day?

> Sharing what Jesus has done in our life.
> Encouraging someone who is struggling.
> Checking on someone who is sick.
> Giving someone a ride to the store.
> Driving a shut-in to a Bible study or church.

People who, despite their hardships, handle challenges by putting their faith into action inspire me.

These are people who…

> are not consumed by their own struggle.
> keep their eyes on Jesus.
> know in their heart God is in control of their lives.
> remain positive.
> don't blame God for "bad" things.
> count their blessings.
> are honest with God.
> know God is their strength.

Christine M. Fisher

embrace God's promises.

know God's grace is greater than what they are facing.

I texted a friend three simple words: Faith in action. These words described what I saw in the lives of her and her adult daughter. For over nine years, my friend has dealt with the debilitating, chronic illness of Crohn's disease. She never knows when it will flare up, making her housebound despite plans she might have. She doesn't look sick, so it can be difficult for others to understand. To complicate her life, she recently learned she has arthritis. Some days she can barely get out of bed and may need the assistance of a walker.

She has four children. The eldest is a young adult who has had several health issues through the years, including diabetes. Recently, they learned she most likely has a brain tumor. In my text, I asked how her daughter was dealing with this news. My friend replied, "She is in good spirits. Praise the Lord!" Even in their frustration, as they cry out to Him, honestly expressing their feelings to their Father, there is healing. They continue to cling to God and turn their situations over to Him. Below are some thoughts my friend shared that speak volumes of her faith in action.

> "I surrender all, Lord. I'm feeling as if everything is happening at once and I can't do it on my own. This load is too heavy so, here it is! Thank You for being my strength and carrying me when I can't walk the road on my own. Because of You and Your promises, I don't have to!

> "It's the frightened whisper of my momma heart as I repeat, 'I do believe, help me in my unbelief!' Lord, I boldly come before you, asking for Your intervention. So many things are happening that it's hard to breathe. Please make Your presence known and help me leave it all with You!

"As I pray for my oldest child and bring my concerns to the Throne, I take comfort that she is His child, and He loves her even more than I ever could!

"People need to stop saying, 'at least I can pray.' Prayer is the most powerful thing a person can do because you are literally handing the situation over to the God of miracles. Be grateful Jesus paved the way for us to speak with our Maker, our Heavenly Father! And pray!

"We're going through some difficult things, but there's also good things as well. Trusting God with and through it. He'll get us through!

"God definitely has this all in His more than capable hands. I'm trusting Him by letting it all go. Every single piece of this, I am handing over to Him. Whatever He has planned is going to be something huge. So go, God! I can't wait to see what You are going to do."

I see faith in action in the way my friend and her daughter are handling these difficulties. Their faith inspires me to have a better attitude about things in life, and to see how I can grow more in my faith.

I believe this quote sums up her philosophy of life:

"Gratitude produces deep, abiding joy because we know God is working in us, even through difficulties." –Charles Stanley

"Dear children, let's not merely say that we love each other; let us show the truth by our actions."
~ 1 John 3:18 (NLT)

Christine M. Fisher

9

My Utmost Respect

Recently my cousin's daughter went through basic training for the Air Force. My cousin agonized for days waiting and wondering how her daughter was doing. Her daughter did very well, and it was great when the family reunited.

My youngest son has a friend he's known since they were six years old. After graduating high school, this young man joined the Air Force. I thought of him and his family while he was in basic training. Cell phone use is banned during boot camp to help trainees stay focused. Being separated had to be difficult.

The entire family makes sacrifices. Parents and siblings are left to wonder how their loved one is doing and are often separated for long periods of time. The young adult makes sacrifices to serve our country and protect our freedom. They face the possibility of being deployed and often see destruction or death during their tour of service. What a huge sacrifice.

Attending my niece's Police Academy graduation made me think about going into such a profession. Thinking about the work she will be doing is a bit intimidating. I give her credit for wanting to work in a profession of protecting lives and seeking justice. Watching a video of her six-month "boot camp" opened my eyes to the reality of what is endured.

Surviving boot camp is a great achievement in all areas of service. They should be proud of their accomplishments. I offer a sincere thank you to those who have served in any capacity, from our past, present, and future. I also salute your families for their sacrifices. You have my utmost respect. May God bless you and keep you safe.

God knows how these people and their families feel.

God chose the ultimate sacrifice in sending His only Son, Jesus to earth. God sent Jesus to live and serve somewhere else for a time, though God was always with Him.

Jesus willingly sacrificed His own life, choosing to die on the cross for you and me, to carry out God's will. Yes, Jesus put His life on the line for you and me! I am so thankful for that ultimate sacrifice.

"This is how we know what love is: Jesus Christ laid down his life for us. And we ought to lay down our lives for our brothers and sisters."
~ 1 John 3:16

10

Choices

God has given us free will, which applies to both simple, daily choices and long-lasting life-altering choices, which impact the kingdom of God.

Life is filled with choices. There are the simple, daily choices like what we wear, what we eat, and what we do next.

> What about the choices that have deeper, lasting effects?
> When we have a debilitating disease or when we have a child who strays from the path, how do we deal with it?
> When the chips are down and things appear hopeless, what do we do then?

We are better off when we choose to handle our trials with a positive, encouraging attitude. It does no good to be negative and blame others for our problems.

I encourage you, in the midst of life's difficult events and circumstances, choose to...

> look at the positive.
> be in a good mood.
> take the higher road.
> step outside your comfort zone.
> live fully.
> love all.
> extend forgiveness.
> be kind.
> pray for all.

encourage others.

be there for those who might be alone.

draw closer to God.

build others up.

speak life.

live by faith.

Attitude, after all, is everything.

Let's impact the kingdom of God together.

"This day I call the heavens and earth as witnesses against you that I have set before you life and death, blessings and curses. Now choose life, so that you and your children may live and that you may love the Lord your God, listen to his voice, and hold fast to him. For the Lord is your life…"

~ Deuteronomy 30:19-20

Christine M. Fisher

11

Legacy

I attended the funeral of a dear friend who suffered greatly the last few weeks of his life. Before his death, I saw how his wife, so patiently and lovingly, cared for him. During his last six days, their son kept vigil 24/7 at his hospital bedside. Their loving example has blessed and enriched my life.

It is difficult watching someone who is facing death. We can ask the Lord to restore and heal them, but if that does not happen, we can still show Christ's love and compassion to them. It's amazing when people who are suffering end up ministering to us as we try to support them. When this happens, I am encouraged to live out my faith even more powerfully.

Attending funerals is also difficult. It is hard to know what to say. I'm learning the best thing is to say something like, "I am sorry for your loss. I am praying for you." Sometimes our presence and hugs show we care, which can be better than words.

At funerals, we often share about the legacy of the deceased person. We talk about the difference or impact the person had on our life. Sharing these memories and influences help keep the memories alive and offer comfort to the family.

Have you thought about the legacy you are leaving? Let's leave a legacy that will make a difference for others.

I hope my life reflects…

> sharing Christ's love with others.
> having a servant's heart.

blessing others by helping them, even in the small things.

being an encourager in Christ.

living a prayerful life.

sharing Christ in the simple, ordinary things through my writings.

showing kindness and respect to others.

putting faith in God.

being a good listener.

being a dependable friend.

Think about what you are leaving for others. Is there anything you want to do differently? If so, it's not too late to start making changes.

"And await the mercy of our Lord Jesus Christ, who will bring you eternal life. In this way, you will keep yourselves safe in God's love."
~ Jude 1:21 (NLT)

Christine M. Fisher

12

A Journey of Growth

A text from my youngest son away at college, asked, "What are you up to?" I knew this wasn't a good sign, as it was a few hours after he was to attend a meeting. I phoned him right away, taking a deep breath.

His first words were, "How is your faith?" I replied, "Well, usually strong until something 'big' comes along. Then it seems my faith can be easily shaken or weakened."

During the ten-minute conversation, he encouraged my faith by his outlook. His attitude exemplified one of faith, knowing that however God worked things out, he would make the best of it. My son was trusting in God's sovereign will.

After our phone call, I headed to church. As only God can do, I saw my Pastor, which is an encounter that had not happened before. Since he asked how I was, I voiced my concern about my son. I shared how, sometimes when a major crisis arises, my faith seems to vanish. His reply was, "The faith is in you. I will be praying for your son." His words were a great encouragement. I dug into my soul to find the faith to trust in God. Throughout the following days, I kept thinking about the question my son first asked on the phone call, "How is your faith?"

God had my attention when I read this version of a familiar story:

"One day Jesus said to his disciples, 'Let us go over to the other side of the lake.' So they got into a boat and set out. As they sailed, he fell asleep. A squall came down on the lake, so that the boat was being swamped, and they were in great danger. The disciples went and woke him, saying, 'Master,

Master, we're going to drown!' He got up and rebuked the wind and the raging waters; the storm subsided, and all was calm. 'Where is your faith?' he asked his disciples. In fear and amazement they asked one another, 'Who is this? He commands even the winds and the water, and they obey him.'"
~ Luke 8:22-25

The question Jesus asked his disciples, *"Where is your faith?"* reminded me of my son's question. This story gave me comfort as I reread it the following days. The disciples, who spent so much time with Jesus, still had fear and doubts just as we often do. How often does fear take the place of faith?

The way this situation played out reminded me of the importance of...

> the role others play in our faith.
>> Talking with my Pastor encouraged me to dig deeper into my faith. Knowing he was praying for my son brought me peace. Having prayer warriors praying through the tough times is a great comfort.

> putting in time alone with the Lord.
>> Seeking the Lord and His will and finding the passage from Luke 8 helped me come to acceptance no matter the outcome. The more time we spend with God, the more we encounter His presence.

> remembering and knowing Jesus is with us working everything out.
>> Reading scripture and praying continually, even praising the Lord through the storms, are ways we come to know Jesus is always with us. Even when things don't go the way we think they should, Jesus is still working everything out.

God was gracious. After a second meeting, everything turned out favorably for my son. We were grateful and pleasantly surprised. This journey was another stepping-stone of growing in trust and faith, leaning into God, and knowing His plan is best.

As you go about life, never underestimate the impact the simplest of encounters and statements can have in your life. Keep growing in trust and faith, knowing God provides what you need when you need it. Remember what a precious gift it is to be Christ for others in their time of need.

"…Supplement your faith with a generous provision of moral excellence, and moral excellence with knowledge, and knowledge with self-control, and self-control with patient endurance, and patient endurance with godliness, and godliness with brotherly affection, and brotherly affection with love for everyone."
~ 2 Peter 1:5-7 (NLT)

13

God Friended Me

One day some friends mentioned a television show entitled, *God Friended Me.*

The main character, Miles, is a part-time podcaster. He is an outspoken atheist despite being the son of a minister. One day Miles receives a friend request on Facebook from God. At first, he declines the request, but through a series of events, finally accepts.

Each episode is about God sending Miles a friend request name that he and some friends are to help. They act as detectives researching and piecing together links of information to help the person. These situations cause Miles to wrestle with his faith and often bring him closer to his father. His friends feel great helping others, and their lives are changed because of their willingness to extend themselves.

This television show made me think about some of the concepts we can apply to our daily lives.

Have you accepted God's friend request in your life? God is always waiting for us to be His friend. He won't force Himself on us, but He longs for us.

"No longer do I call you servants, for the servant does not know
what his master is doing; but I have called you friends, for all that
I have heard from my Father I have made known to you."
~ John 15:15 (ESV)

What if we look at each person we encounter as a friend suggestion sent by God? Every person God puts in our path is an opportunity. Our lives are to be lived in community, showing ourselves friendly.

"Two people are better off than one, for they can help each other succeed. If one person falls, the other can reach out and help. But someone who falls alone is in real trouble."
~ Ecclesiastes 4:9-10 (NLT)

Do you see how every interaction and situation in life are related and have a ripple effect? One small comment or gesture can change one life at a time, having a ripple effect for either good or evil.

"For not only has the word of the Lord sounded forth from you in Macedonia and Achaia, but your faith in God has gone forth everywhere, so that we need not say anything."
~ 1 Thessalonians 1:8 (ESV)

Why wouldn't God use you to help others? Isn't it a big part of our purpose to help others in whatever way we can? Didn't Jesus give us that example?

"I tell you the truth, anyone who believes in me will do the same works I have done, and even greater works, because I am going to be with the Father."
~ John 14:12 (NLT)

Do you see how your life is better through helping others? Through helping others, have you experienced how it is more blessed to give than to receive?

"And I have been a constant example of how you can help those in need by working hard. You should remember the words of the Lord Jesus: 'It is more blessed to give than to receive.'"
~ Acts 20:35 (NLT)

"Keep on loving each other as brothers and sisters. Don't forget to show hospitality to strangers, for some who have done this have entertained angels without realizing it!"
~ Hebrews 13:1-2 (NLT)

14

Simple Acts

We never know when the smallest act of kindness can have the biggest impact on someone else.

Despite being a non-clinical hospital employee, I am annually required to obtain a tuberculin (TB) test. It only takes a few seconds to administer the test and to make sure I am up-to-date on my immunizations.

I arrived at the office a few minutes before it opened and was second in line. The first nurse took the first employee. A second nurse called the lady standing behind me saying, "I assume you were first in line since your paper was first." The lady behind me seemed a little confused. I told her it was okay to go ahead of me. A few extra minutes of waiting was no problem.

When done, the lady poked her head in the office and thanked me for letting her go first. The nurse also thanked me and apologized for the confusion, saying how nice that I let the lady go first.

Two days later, I returned for the results of the TB test. Much to my surprise, the lady who went ahead of me on the first day was coming down the hallway. She already had her results. She thanked me again and shared, "I was sitting in the hallway two days ago because of an issue with my leg. Standing in line was too difficult. When the nurse called my name, I was caught off guard and just got up and went. I said a silent prayer of blessing for you, thankful for your simple act of kindness."

It was a good reminder that we just never know what people may be dealing with and how a small, simple act of kindness may bless another.

"Be devoted to one another in love. Honor one another above yourselves."
~ Romans 12:10

15

Glorifying the Lord

"Go in peace, glorifying the Lord by your life." Our Pastor says this at the end of every service. It is a powerful reminder of how we should live daily until we are called home to heaven.

What examples of glorifying the Lord can we learn from the life of Jesus?

JESUS RESPECTED THE LOWLY, CHOOSING SOME TO BE HIS FIRST FOLLOWERS

"One day as Jesus was walking along the shore of the Sea of Galilee, he saw two brothers—Simon, also called Peter, and Andrew—throwing a net into the water, for they fished for a living. Jesus called out to them, 'Come, follow me, and I will show you how to fish for people!'"
~ Matthew 4:18-19 (NLT)

JESUS BEFRIENDED SINNERS

"While Jesus was having dinner at Matthew's house, many tax collectors and sinners came and ate with him and his disciples."
~ Matthew 9:10

JESUS CALLED PEOPLE TO REPENTANCE

"From that time on Jesus began to preach, 'Repent, for the kingdom of heaven has come near.'"
~ Matthew 4:17

JESUS BROKE THE SOCIAL RULES OF THE DAY TO SHOW GOD'S UNCONDITIONAL LOVE FOR ALL

"Soon a Samaritan woman came to draw water, and Jesus said to her, 'Please give me a drink.' He was alone at the time because his disciples had gone into the village to buy some food. The woman was surprised, for Jews refuse to have anything to do with Samaritans. She said to Jesus, 'You are a Jew, and I am a Samaritan woman. Why are you asking me for a drink?' Jesus replied, 'If you only knew the gift God has for you and who you are speaking to, you would ask me, and I would give you living water.'"
~ John 4:7-10 (NLT)

JESUS ENGAGED THE LITTLE CHILDREN SHOWING HIS GREAT LOVE FOR THEM

"But Jesus said, 'Let the children come to me. Don't stop them! For the Kingdom of Heaven belongs to those who are like these children.' And he placed his hands on their heads and blessed them before he left."
~ Matthew 19:14-15 (NLT)

JESUS HEALED THE PHYSICALLY ILL

"Great crowds came to him, bringing the lame, the blind, the crippled, the mute and many others, and laid them at his feet; and he healed them."
~ Matthew 15:30

JESUS SHARED GRACE (UNMERITED FAVOR) AND MERCY (LOVING-KINDNESS)

"A man with leprosy came and knelt before him and said, 'Lord, if you are willing, you can make me clean.' Jesus reached out his hand and touched the man. 'I am willing,' he said. 'Be clean!' Immediately he was cleansed of his leprosy."
~ Matthew 8:2-3

Christine M. Fisher

JESUS MODELED BEING A HUMBLE SERVANT

"After washing their feet, he put on his robe again and sat down and asked, 'Do you understand what I was doing?'"
~ John 13:12 (NLT)

JESUS FORGAVE EVEN THOSE WHO PUT HIM TO DEATH

"And Jesus said, 'Father, forgive them, for they know not what they do.' And they cast lots to divide his garments."
~ Luke 23:34 (ESV)

JESUS DEMONSTRATED COMPASSION

"A funeral procession was coming out as he approached the village gate. The young man who had died was a widow's only son, and a large crowd from the village was with her. When the Lord saw her, his heart overflowed with compassion. 'Don't cry!' he said. Then he walked over to the coffin and touched it, and the bearers stopped. 'Young man,' he said, 'I tell you, get up.' Then the dead boy sat up and began to talk! And Jesus gave him back to his mother."
~ Luke 7:12-15 (NLT)

JESUS EXEMPLIFIED OBEDIENCE

Truly, the ultimate way Jesus glorified God was in His obedience to Him even to the point of death on the cross.

"Then Jesus left them a second time and prayed, 'My Father! If this cup cannot be taken away unless I drink it, your will be done.'"
~ Matthew 26:42 (NLT)

"After saying all these things, Jesus looked up to heaven and said, 'Father, the hour has come. Glorify your Son so he can give glory back to you.'"
~ John 17:1 (NLT)

Glorifying the Lord is the reason we are on this earth. Jesus' life is the model we are privileged to emulate each day.

Our lives are a daily call to fulfill that mission with…

> the attitude of our heart.
> our actions.
> the love we share with all!

Be encouraged to awake each day and let your prayer be, "God, fill me with your peace. Please let my life glorify you. Let me be your instrument." Try and focus on this prayer throughout the day and go do amazing things.

"Not to us, O Lord, not to us, but to your name goes all the glory for your unfailing love and faithfulness."
~ Psalm 115:1 (NLT)

Christine M. Fisher

16

A Heartfelt Note

My twenty-fifth Mother's Day was special. It was a surprise to receive a gift card in the mail from my oldest son who moved out of state the year before. It was the first gift he ever gave me. Gifts have never been a top contender of the five love languages in our house. His thoughtfulness and act of kindness touched my heart. The gift card read, "To Mom, from Dallas. Happy Mother's Day from your favorite child."

That same Mother's Day, my younger son was up early. I heard noises coming from the kitchen as he prepared his usual "big teen" breakfast. The day before, I told him, "I wish I could eat what you do! But I can't, since I'm not a growing teen and don't work out with the intensity you do." But on that special day, much to my surprise, he treated me to a "big teen" breakfast.

The note he gave me along with my breakfast brought tears to my eyes. "Thank you for everything you do for me. From cooking, to driving, caring for, and loving me. You're the best mother there is, and I appreciate you. No matter what happens or how I act on a certain day, know that I love you and celebrate everyday like it's Mother's Day/your birthday. Love, Caleb (your favorite child)."

His words were the best part of the breakfast, for sure. On a side note, being the "favorite" is a running joke in our family. Caleb wrote "your favorite child" because he saw it on the present from his older brother the day before. Both boys think they are the favorite; my daughter always says, "I'm the angel." I think it's great they know how special they are.

Later that day, I thought of the words he wrote and what a good parallel to our relationship with God, our Father.

Do we take time to thank God for everything He does for us?

He doesn't cook for us or drive us around, but He does provide the...

> food we eat.
> means to buy or grow the food.
> knowledge to get an education.
> ability to work to provide for and support our family.
> different modes of transportation to get wherever we wish and can afford.
> land on which we live.
> beautiful nature around us.
> places and ways to worship Him.
> communities of people who love and care for us.

Do we take time to thank God for all the ways He cares for us in...

> providing us with solace when we need it?
> orchestrating a song on the radio that ministers to our soul?
> sending a beautiful sunset to see His radiance?
> reading a Bible verse that shows His perfect timing?

Do we take time to thank God for loving us more than anyone in the world can or does?

He...

> loves us unconditionally, no matter what we do.
> is the ultimate best Father there is.
> is always with us, never leaves us, and lives within us.

Give thanks to God continually for all He does. Intentionally celebrate each day, no matter the circumstances.

"A new command I give you: Love one another.
As I have loved you, so you must love one another."
~ John 13:34

17

Spreading Light

"There are two ways of spreading light—to be the candle
or the mirror that reflects it."
–Edith Wharton

The above quote caught my eye. There are different ways of interpreting it depending on your focus. Here's my interpretation.

First, let's define light, using two Bible verses as a reference point.

*"This is the message we have heard from him and declare to you:
God is light; in him there is no darkness at all."*
~ 1 John 1:5

*"When Jesus spoke again to the people, he said, 'I am the light of the world.
Whoever follows me will never walk in darkness,
but will have the light of life.'"*
~ John 8:12

In reading these two Bible verses, we learn that God is light and Jesus is the light of the world. How perfect that we can say, "Like Father, like Son!"

Now, let me rewrite the quote: "There are two ways of spreading God and Jesus—to be the candle or the mirror that reflects them."

Did you catch the ending of John 8:12? If we follow Jesus, we will have the light of life. What an honor and privilege. Could that light represent the candle or mirror from the quote?

Christine M. Fisher

Think about a candle. It needs a source to get it started. In this case, the source is none other than God and Jesus. Once lit, the candle continues to shine brightly because of the source: God and Jesus. As we keep feeding that source, through reading Scripture, praying, fellowship with other believers, the flame continues to shine brightly.

The candle...

        emits light into the darkness.
        casts shadows on other's lives.
        lights other people's candles.
        warms other's lives.
        never gets dim even with lighting other's candles.
        illuminates the path.

The mirror...

        reflects what is there.
        brings awareness to our lives.
        reflects the truth.
        if living sinfully, will reflect darkness.
        if living for God and Jesus, will reflect light.
        reflects light in a proportional way to the original object: The light of God and Jesus.

Be encouraged to be both the candle and the mirror in spreading the light of God and Jesus to others!

> *"It was not by their sword that they won the land, nor did their arm bring them victory; it was your right hand, your arm, and the light of your face, for you loved them."*
> ~ Psalm 44:3

18

Family

How do you define family? Maybe your first response would be "blood related people who are near and dear to me."

That is true, but I believe there is an even deeper definition for family. Today, families are scattered around the country, away from one another, so finding family is more important than ever.

In a Google search for definitions of family, I thought this one was perfect, from the Milton Hershey School website. An alumnus shared this thought:

> "I've learned over the years that what defines family is not solely blood relation. Family consists of the people who support and love you, and the people you can confide in and trust."[1]

Is your definition of family those people who...

> love you?
> support you?
> you can confide in?
> you can trust?

A friend of mine is a dance instructor. She agrees the dance teachers and students consider each other family. This was evident at a dance recital during the slide show of the graduating seniors. They support, love, confide in, and trust each other.

What are some other possible examples of family?

Perhaps it's people from…

> your workplace.
> a sports team.
> your neighborhood.
> your church.
> support groups.
> musical organizations.
> social media.
> small groups.

As newlyweds, my husband and I reached out to couples from church to get together for food and fellowship. We were family to some who did not have relatives in the area. When we started having families of our own, we continued to support each other. Little by little, most of them moved away. As our family grew and life became busier, it was more difficult to find others and take time to fellowship.

Our youngest son plays baseball year-round. We call one of the coaches his "adopted dad," as he loves and cares for my son the same way he does his own. My son and I attended this coach's team championship game. A few parents wished my son well in college. When my son was not with me at a game, people asked about him. I had not met many of them before. What a great family of people to support and love my son.

Think about Jesus' short life on earth. I believe the twelve disciples were family to Him. They were a community that supported, loved, confided in, and trusted each other. Recall that even Jesus' blood family didn't think He was the Messiah.

Take a few minutes to reflect on what family means to you.

> Can you identify who is family in your life?
> Who are you reaching out to be family to?

Isn't life brighter when we are family to one another?

Doesn't it make us think less of ourselves and more of others?

It is as simple as encouraging a friend who is having a bad day or asking someone how you can pray for them.

One week I was blessed to get messages from two people saying I was their biggest cheerleader. Receiving a text from a person I have never met, letting me know a coworkers surgery went well, made me smile. She knew I cared. For me, they all represent family.

You know what? It is "being church" to others, and that is our true calling. How awesome is that? May I encourage you to not just go to church; be the church.

"Honor your father and mother. Love your neighbor as yourself."
~ Matthew 19:19 (NLT)

19

Change the World

While on vacation, there was one day the ocean had lots of floating seaweed. As I was cooling off in the water, I noticed a young boy collecting the seaweed and putting it on an inflatable float. He would then wade the float to shore and dump the seaweed on the beach. He made several trips back and forth. Though I can't be sure of his motive, I think his actions qualify as a random act of kindness. He was changing the world, making the water seaweed-free for people to enjoy.

What the boy did not know was how his random act of kindness inspired others to add a few sprigs of seaweed to his pile. This child, in the seaweed water, was doing what he could where he was. He was living the saying,

> "Do what you can with all you have wherever you are."
> –T. Roosevelt

How do we change the world? One random act of kindness at a time. As the saying goes, "Actions speak louder than words."

You can make the world a better place for even one person or animal. One act of kindness can change someone's world. Find what you can do, in whatever circumstance you find yourself in, wherever you are. Actively seek those ways and act on them.

> *"Don't let anyone think less of you because you are young.*
> *Be an example to all believers in what you say, in the way*
> *you live, in your love, your faith, and your purity."*
> ~ 1 Timothy 4:12 (NLT)

20

Show Thyself Friendly

We received an email from my youngest son's teacher:

> "Hi, I wanted to let you know what a treat it is to have your son in my class. He has taken it upon himself to be the official greeter. He stands in the doorway and welcomes each student with a firm handshake and a hardy 'welcome to class!' It's interesting to see how the other students react. They say hello and return the handshake, almost always with a smile. I don't know what inspired him to do this, but I love it! It sets a positive tone for the entire class and helps remind us that we're all in this together. You have quite a remarkable son!"

Her words brought a tear to my eye and made me think how the little things mean so much. When I asked my son what inspired him to do this, he responded:

> "I am one of the first people to get to the classroom. I know you need a good attitude to spread happiness to others. So I was inspired to make people happy by greeting them at the door."

A few days later, he shared another story.

In the same class, a girl walked in looking sad. My son asked why she was sad and threw her a floral lei he had been wearing, saying her day was going to get better. She said, "I don't know," and sat down. When my son finished greeting everyone, he sat in an empty chair beside the girl. She said she was still feeling down because she was dwelling on something sad. Partway through class, he threw his second lei over her head, which made her laugh.

My son then proceeded to take off his floral Hawaiian shirt (yes, he had a shirt under it) and tossed it to the girl. He said, "When you wear a floral shirt, you can't be sad." She put the shirt on over her clothes. Later she told him, "It was then I started having a good day. Thank you."

> "What counts in life is not the mere fact that we have lived. It is the difference we have made to the lives of others that will determine the significance of the life we lead." –Nelson Mandela

> Do you take time to make people feel welcome?
> Do you notice when others are sad and try to cheer them up?
> Do you take action in filling a need?
> Is there something creative or outside your comfort zone you can do to brighten someone's day?

It's great to see the ripple effect of showing thyself friendly.

The teacher shared two of the benefits she observed from my sons actions. First, he set a positive tone and, second, it was a reminder of how we are all in this together.

We should be there for others to create a positive and loving environment, reflecting Christ to all.

I recently had the delightful experience of meeting a coworker for lunch. We communicate via email since our workplaces are an hour apart. We had a wonderful time talking and sharing for almost three hours. Both of our lives have been enriched by showing ourselves friendly in caring for one another.

How can you show thyself friendly? We can all make a difference and brighten another's day. As Christians, we should be continually sharing the light of Christ through our words and actions. It is because of Christ in our heart and the love He has for us, we can't help but extend Him to others.

> *"The aim of our charge is love that issues from a pure heart*
> *and a good conscience and a sincere faith."*
> ~ 1 Timothy 1:5 (ESV)

21

Stepping Out in Faith

Do you ever step out in faith, seizing the moment, to do what suddenly pops in your head, knowing it is part of a divine plan? After all, our lives are not really our own; everything we have and are belongs to God.

As I pulled into Dunkin Donuts, I thought, "I should pay it forward." So, I told the drive-thru cashier I wanted to pay for the car behind me. He gladly took my money. It felt good to do something I had never done before. I stepped out in faith, trusting my instinct to obey the prompting.

A few days later, I went back to the drive-thru of Dunkin Donuts. The same cashier was there to take my money, except this time, he told me my order was already paid for. I was surprised. I reminded him that I "paid it forward" a few days earlier. He replied, "I remember. The day you started it, there was a chain reaction of six or seven cars." How amazing is that? What an inspiring God moment that went full circle.

Another day, I was driving and saw an older gentleman carrying a backpack and a few bags of groceries. He stopped to adjust the load as he was hobbling along the street. The thought of asking if he needed a ride popped in my head. I pulled into a church parking lot and debated whether I should go back. I found myself clearing off the passenger seat and headed back. When I spotted him, he was still struggling with his bags. I rolled down the window and asked him if he wanted a ride. He thanked me for not hitting him (I hope he didn't think I was a bad driver), and said he was good. He shared that he recently had hip surgery and needed to get the kinks in his back worked out. I double-checked once more before leaving, adding a "God bless you."

I believe Jesus would have done the same thing if He were driving and saw the gentleman. Even though he did not accept the ride, he may have realized someone cared. For me, I am learning to step out in faith and obey the voice of God.

My husband and I were waiting in the self-checkout line of a grocery store when we saw a man trying to pay for his items. We could see the screen said, "Credit card denied." He was trying another card when a register became available for us. I asked my husband if we should pay for the man's order. He said he thought about it too, but we hesitated. After we checked out, the man was still at his register, so my husband asked him if he could pay for it. The man said, "Sure," shook my husband's hand, and thanked him. Again, it's not something we had done before. However, seeing someone in need, stepping out in faith, and doing what Jesus would do was the right thing.

Make every interaction count, even the small ones. They are all relevant.

"We remember before our God and Father your work produced by faith, your labor prompted by love, and your endurance inspired by hope in our Lord Jesus Christ."
~ 1 Thessalonians 1:3

Section 2

GOD'S LOVE ILLUMINATED IN SCRIPTURE

"There is no greater love than to lay down one's life for one's friends."
~ John 15:13 (NLT)

God shared His love with us by sending His one and only Son, Jesus, as an atoning sacrifice for our sins. It is His plan of redemption for us so we can spend eternity in heaven.

Scripture is God's love story for all humanity. We owe it all to Jesus who willingly laid down His life for His friends. It is the greatest expression of love for you and me. What a privilege we have to be called friends of Jesus.

God's love illuminated in Scripture.

22

The Heart

*"When they arrived, Samuel took one look at Eliab and thought,
'Surely this is the Lord's anointed!' But the Lord said to Samuel,
'Don't judge by his appearance or height, for I have rejected him.
The Lord doesn't see things the way you see them. People judge
by outward appearance, but the Lord looks at the heart.'"*
~ 1 Samuel 16:6-7 (NLT)

This passage reveals what is important to God. God cares most about the condition of our heart. His thoughts and ways are different from ours. He is reminding us that the outward things - our looks, careers, money, how we compare to others - are not what matters to Him.

The saying, "Don't judge a book by its cover," goes along with this scripture and literally hit home when I saw the printed cover of my first published book, *God's Presence Illuminated*. You can probably envision my enthusiasm and excitement when I opened the first shipment of books. When I saw the cover, my heart sank. The rising sun coming up over the ocean had a green glow around it instead of the yellow glow in the original picture I had taken.

I was excited to get copies into the hands of people, but I wanted the cover to display the picture I knew it should be. To make matters worse, the printing company said the cover would be corrected, and they would expedite a new order. An email a few days later negated that offer, so I was stuck with the green glow books.

People tried to encourage me by sharing the Biblical significance of green. It is related to praise, growth, prosperity, new beginnings, restoration, harmony, and everlasting life. Green is also the color of nature at its finest and is symbolic of resurrection, which we see each spring. Some people didn't notice the green glow. Another said when taking a picture of the sun, a green glow is often present. I was grateful for the encouragement.

Through this, I was reminded that the contents and message of a book are more important than the cover. It is just as the condition of our heart is more important to God than our outward appearance or circumstances.

Take time to consider the condition of your heart.

> Is your heart hardened toward God or is it full of God's love and goodness?
> Is your heart full of pride and sin?
> Do your actions reflect a heart of love or a heart of corruption?
> Do you love God and people more than you love material things?
> Do your actions reflect a healthy heart that reflects God's Word?
> Do you serve others with joy, helping the poor and marginalized?
> Do you judge others by their physical appearance?

Seek to emulate God's love by looking at people's hearts, not their outward appearance. Take time to get to know people, understand them, and see what kind of fruit their lives produce. With an open heart, walk in love and focus on the heart of those in your path.

> *"This is my commandment: Love each other in*
> *the same way I have loved you."*
> ~ John 15:12 (NLT)

23

Fishers of Men

During a Sunday outing to a state park, I observed several people fishing from the shoreline. Some people came and left without catching anything. A couple of men were there for over three hours. I overheard them say they caught fish numbers seven and eight. Only those who stayed the longest were rewarded, which took my thoughts to the Sea of Galilee with Jesus and His disciples.

> *"While walking by the Sea of Galilee, he saw two brothers, Simon (who is called Peter) and Andrew his brother, casting a net into the sea, for they were fishermen. And he said to them, 'Follow me, and I will make you fishers of men.' Immediately they left their nets and followed him."*
> ~ Matthew 4:18-20 (ESV)

I thought about how, in our lives, the privilege of being fishers of men is relatable to fishing.

The basic steps to fishing are bait the line, cast the line, reel in the line, repeat the sequence.

Consider how the fishing pole can be symbolic of our lives, while the fish represent the people in our lives. Our bait is the fruit of the Spirit – love, peace, kindness, goodness, gentleness, even compassion, which we cast out into the sea of life. As we cast our bait, ripples are created in the water spreading goodness to the multitudes. Sometimes when we cast our line, it gets stuck on something. Our life might need a little redirection. Sometimes our line does not go far in the water. Maybe we need a little more strength or encouragement to gain confidence. We reel the people in, to a closer relationship with Jesus, blessing one person at a time. Our goal is to keep casting the line, using our bait of love to show the Light of Christ. Keep repeating the sequence, being true fishers of men.

Just as the men were happy when they reeled in another fish, our lives are filled with joy and excitement as we touch lives in Jesus' name. We need to be patient in fishing for men. We might not see results right away, but we need to live faithfully. We never know when something we say or do may influence another's life. The fishermen who stayed the longest, waiting with patient expectation, received the reward.

> *"When he had finished speaking, he said to Simon, 'Now go out where it is deeper, and let down your nets to catch some fish.' 'Master,' Simon replied, 'We worked hard all last night and didn't catch a thing. But if you say so, I'll let the nets down again.' And this time their nets were so full of fish they began to tear!"*
> ~ Luke 5:4-6 (NLT)

Ponder the fact that Jesus, the Savior of the world, called simple ordinary people, most of them fishermen, as His first followers. Jesus did not choose the richest nor the most famous or powerful ones to be His closest friends. Notice how, after Jesus died, His earliest disciples went back to fishing, even though Jesus told them they would be "fishers of men."

> *"Simon Peter, Thomas (called the Twin), Nathanael of Cana in Galilee, the sons of Zebedee, and two others of his disciples were together. Simon Peter said to them, 'I am going fishing.' They said to him, 'We will go with you.' They went out and got into the boat, but that night they caught nothing."*
> ~ John 21:2-3 (ESV)

Before His resurrection, Jesus told His disciples:

*"But you will receive power when the Holy Spirit comes upon you.
And you will be my witnesses, telling people about me everywhere—in
Jerusalem, throughout Judea, in Samaria, and to the ends of the earth."*
~ Acts 1:8 (NLT)

He reminded them of their true calling, which was to be fishers of men, proclaiming the Good News everywhere and to everyone. God calls us, simple ordinary people, to be fishers of men, proclaiming the Good News of Jesus in our little ways. Fishing for men is our highest calling, our mission, and we have the Holy Spirit working in and through us to fulfill this mission.

How are you living out your highest calling to be a fisher of men?

*"Now that you have purified yourselves by obeying the truth so that you
have sincere love for each other, love one another deeply, from the heart."*
~ 1 Peter 1:22

24

Off the Beaten Path

"For I have stayed on God's paths; I have followed
his ways and not turned aside."
~ Job 23:11 (NLT)

"You make known to me the path of life; in your presence there is
fullness of joy; at your right hand are pleasures forevermore."
~ Psalm 16:11 (ESV)

"Mark out a straight path for your feet; stay on the safe path.
Don't get sidetracked; keep your feet from following evil."
~ Proverbs 4:26-27 (NLT)

One fall, I was walking through the woods, in unfamiliar territory, looking for a path I thought led to an open field. The hike was challenging with so many leaves strewn over the trail. I went further than I should have and stopped at what appeared to be a dead-end. Getting lost in the woods added to the meaning of the phrase "off the beaten path."

Think about your life before you came to know and love Christ. Were you off the beaten path with the way you were living? Maybe your lifestyle was one of lying, stealing, cheating, drunkenness, carousing, sexual immorality, or any combination of these things. What happened to change your life?

I imagine, at your lowest point, God used something to cause you to have a "metanoia" conversion. A Biblical synonym, especially referenced in the New Testament, for the word metanoia is "repentance." Other synonyms are: A change of heart, born again, and reformation. Translated literally, metanoia means a change of one's mind or purpose.

"In those days John the Baptist came preaching in the wilderness of Judea, 'Repent, for the kingdom of heaven is at hand.'"
~ Matthew 3:1-2 (ESV)

In metanoia, we go from living in darkness to light, the Light that is Christ. Jesus is pure light, knowing no darkness. As we follow Him, we, too, have that light, walk in it, and shine His light.

"Again Jesus spoke to them, saying, 'I am the light of the world. Whoever follows me will not walk in darkness, but will have the light of life.'"
~ John 8:12 (ESV)

Even after we have a personal relationship with Christ, it is easy to get off the beaten path.

How many times do we...

> do something we know we shouldn't?
> let negative thoughts take over?
> fail to heed God's voice?
> have unwanted thoughts pop into our mind?

What should we do when this happens?

> Realize we are off the beaten path.
> Confess the error of our way.
> Repent.
> Return to complete metanoia by changing our thinking and ways.
> Return and focus on the Light of Christ and renew our mind with God's Word.

We are on a moment-by-moment journey to eternal life in heaven with our Father, continually changing and striving to improve the way we live. We are not perfect, so each time we mess up is an opportunity to convert our heart and mind back to God. It is a continual process.

> *"Either way, Christ's love controls us. Since we believe that Christ died for all, we also believe that we have all died to our old life."*
> ~ 2 Corinthians 5:14 (NLT)

Christine M. Fisher

25

The Three Greats

"Three things will last forever—faith, hope, and
love—and the greatest of these is love."
~ 1 Corinthians 13:13 (NLT)

A tree is a perfect representation of this verse. A tree's roots, deep in the ground, represent faith. The trunk is representative of hope, followed by the leaves, which represent love.

Faith can be defined as belief, trust, and loyalty to Christ and God. Faith is represented by the roots of the tree, which must be deeply rooted in God, our Creator, and Jesus, His only Son, crucified for you and me. These roots provide our good, solid foundation. Our faith is continually growing, spreading, branching out, and stretching.

"And without faith it is impossible to please God, because
anyone who comes to him must believe that he exists and
that he rewards those who earnestly seek him."
~ Hebrews 11:6

Hope can be defined as trust, a confident assurance in God, the One who fills the hole in our heart. Hope is represented by the tree trunk, always looking and seeing, with our spiritual eyes and our heart. It is seeking how God is working in our lives to benefit us according to His plan, not necessarily ours. Hope brings to life the connection of our faith to God's love.

"This hope is a strong and trustworthy anchor for our souls. It
leads us through the curtain into God's inner sanctuary."
~ Hebrews 6:19 (NLT)

Love is best defined this way. God is love and has demonstrated that love in everything He does. That is indeed the perfect definition. Love, the third great, actually the greatest of the three greats, is represented by the beautiful leaves on a tree.

God's love.
Bringing new life, new birth to our lives.
Shining through us with radiant color.
Renewing us each season.
Spreading His beauty to all those we encounter.

Faith, hope, and love.

Where there is hope, there is faith.
Where there is faith, love happens.

Love is the fruit of the tree; of a life rooted in faith with God, connecting it with hope, the confident assurance we possess in God. Love is the greatest of the greats. Love is triumphant. Love wins!

"For God so loved the world that he gave his one and only Son,
that whoever believes in him shall not perish but have eternal life."
~ John 3:16

Let your roots grow down into God, and let your life be built on Him. Then your faith will grow strong in the truth and you will overflow with thankfulness. Go forth and spread love to all you meet in all you do.

"Be on your guard; stand firm in the faith; be
courageous; be strong. Do everything in love."
~ 1 Corinthians 16:13-14

26

Lessons from the Birds of the Air

Wouldn't it be wonderful to be a bird? How amazing to be free to soar through the sky, back and forth, observing God's beautiful creation, knowing you can find food whenever you are hungry.

At the end of February, I noticed a huge population of robins gathered in yards. My first thought was "the birds of the air." More recently, there have been hawks soaring about. Seeing their wings outstretched reminded me, we are "under the shadow of His wings." Following are a few Bible verses that relate to "the birds of the air" and apply to our lives.

> *"Therefore I tell you, do not worry about your life, what you will eat*
> *or drink; or about your body, what you will wear. Is not life more*
> *important than food, and the body more important than clothes? Look at*
> *the birds of the air; they do not sow or reap or store away in barns, and*
> *yet your heavenly Father feeds them. Are you not much more valuable*
> *than they? Who of you by worrying can add a single hour to his life?"*
> ~ Matthew 6:25-27

God wants us to know we are valuable to Him. Worrying does not add a thing to our life. Let those truths sink into the deepest recess of your heart and soul. To help us realize these truths, Jesus points out how God, our Heavenly Father, takes care of the birds of the air. They live in the present, freely flying around God's beautiful creation. The birds do not store their food to make sure they have enough for a "rainy day."

> *"The birds of the air nest by the waters; they sing among the branches."*
> ~ Psalm 104:12

God reminds us to continually praise Him as we traverse His beautiful creation. We, too, can enjoy the waters God formed, just like the birds that build their nests near the waters. How special to hear the beautiful melodies of different birds singing praises to their Creator.

"Are not two sparrows sold for a penny? Yet not one of them
will fall to the ground apart from the will of your Father. And
even the very hairs of your head are all numbered. So don't
be afraid; you are worth more than many sparrows."
~ Matthew 10:29-31

God reminds us not to be afraid. We are so valuable to Him, He even knows the number of hairs on our head. Even the sparrow is a treasure to God. He loves them so much and knows when one falls to the ground.

"Who provides food for the raven when its young cry out
to God and wander about for lack of food?"
~ Job 38:41

God provides nourishment for us, not only for our body but also for our soul. Yes, God provides for the birds of the air, sending food for them, especially when the young cry out for lack of food. No one or no thing goes without.

"Keep me as the apple of your eye; hide me in the shadow
of your wings from the wicked who are out to destroy
me, from my mortal enemies who surround me."
~ Psalm 17:8-9

In the shadow of God's wings, we are hidden in safety, protected from the wicked. We are the apple of God's eye, so He is our great Protector. We are protected from the wicked who try to attack us. Here are a few Bible verses to help us see how to apply this teaching.

"He will cover you with his feathers, and under his wings you will find refuge; his faithfulness will be your shield and rampart."
~ Psalm 91:4

"Have mercy on me, O God, have mercy on me, for in you my soul takes refuge. I will take refuge in the shadow of your wings until the disaster has passed."
~ Psalm 57:1

"I long to dwell in your tent forever and take refuge in the shelter of your wings."
~ Psalm 61:4

"How priceless is your unfailing love! Both high and low among men find refuge in the shadow of your wings."
~ Psalm 36:7

In the shadow of God's wings, we find refuge. His feathers protect us; His faithfulness is our shield. God's mercy is our refuge and will keep us safe until the disaster has passed. We dwell with God forever in security. His love never fails! He is a refuge for all people.

"Because you are my help, I sing in the shadow of your wings."
~ Psalm 63:7

In the shadow of God's wings, we can sing His praises. Being assured of His help, we have every reason to sing His praises, rejoicing in His goodness.

The next time you are in God's beautiful creation, look for the birds of the sky, smile, and remember how God is reminding you...

of your value,

how He is your refuge protecting you,

every step of the way.

"Let me hear of your unfailing love each morning, for I am trusting you.
Show me where to walk, for I give myself to you."
~ Psalm 143:8 (NLT)

27

Faith of our Friends

Faith is to be lived in "community" with fellow believers where we share experiences, burdens, prayer requests, and encourage one another. We join in thanksgiving to demonstrate God's love. Community comes in different forms. It might be family, friends, a small group from church, or people from cyberspace we have never met in person.

Have you experienced a major crisis where the faith of your friends carried you through? Maybe you could not muster the faith to believe things would turn out okay. Depression, death of a loved one, or living with chronic illness can be debilitating. Perhaps you could not find the strength to pray while enduring your trial. Perhaps it seemed God was distant, even though you know He never leaves us.

When I heard the word "cancer," my life changed in an instant and seemed to come to a standstill. The prayers and support of a few trusted friends pulled me through. I struggled with a big health decision, which resulted in going against "protocol." I know God was leading and guiding me.

Can you think of a time you stepped in to help carry a friend in faith?

When a friend shared that her son was diagnosed with a brain tumor, I asked several friends to join in prayer. I was grateful for more people and prayers to storm heaven on the family's behalf. When she was with her son during treatments, I sent a weekly prayer and Bible verse for encouragement.

There are two Bible stories that demonstrate the importance of faith and how the faith of our friends can intervene for us.

"Some men came, bringing to him a paralyzed man, carried by four of them. Since they could not get him to Jesus because of the crowd, they made an opening in the roof above Jesus by digging through it and then lowered the mat the man was lying on. When Jesus saw their faith, he said to the paralyzed man, 'Son, your sins are forgiven.' Now some teachers of the law were sitting there, thinking to themselves, 'Why does this fellow talk like that? He's blaspheming! Who can forgive sins but God alone?' Immediately Jesus knew in his spirit that this was what they were thinking in their hearts, and he said to them, 'Why are you thinking these things? Which is easier: to say to this paralyzed man, "Your sins are forgiven," or to say, "Get up, take your mat and walk"? But I want you to know that the Son of Man has authority on earth to forgive sins.' So he said to the man, 'I tell you, get up, take your mat and go home.' He got up, took his mat and walked out in full view of them all. This amazed everyone and they praised God, saying, 'We have never seen anything like this!'"
~ Mark 2:3-12

These four men were determined to take their friend to Jesus because they wanted to help him. They were so desperate they made a hole in the roof of the house because the crowds were so great. I love the line, *"When Jesus saw their faith..."* These men stood in faith that Jesus could heal their friend.

Jesus met the man's deepest need of forgiveness first. Jesus then performed another miracle by healing him physically. The man left the house walking, and I have to think, his life continued to reflect the great faith his friends shared that day. The crowd left praising God for the healing.

"There a centurion's servant, whom his master valued highly, was sick and about to die. The centurion heard of Jesus and sent some elders of the Jews to him, asking him to come and heal his servant. When they came to Jesus, they pleaded earnestly with him, 'This man deserves to have you do this, because he loves our nation and has built our synagogue.' So Jesus went with them. He was not far from the house when the centurion sent

*friends to say to him: 'Lord, don't trouble yourself, for I do not deserve
to have you come under my roof. That is why I did not even consider
myself worthy to come to you. But say the word, and my servant will be
healed. For I myself am a man under authority, with soldiers under me.
I tell this one, "Go," and he goes; and that one, "Come," and he comes.
I say to my servant, "Do this," and he does it.' When Jesus heard this, he
was amazed at him, and turning to the crowd following him, he said, 'I
tell you, I have not found such great faith even in Israel.' Then the men
who had been sent returned to the house and found the servant well."*
~ Luke 7:2-10

The centurion, though high in rank, was genuinely concerned about one of
his slaves. The elders stood in faith for the man who was about to die. They
were sent to find Jesus. The centurion knew Jesus was the one who could
save his servant. He respected Jesus' authority. Even though the centurion
was of an elite status, he was humble. He knew Jesus only had to say the
word and his servant would be healed. Jesus rewarded the centurion's faith
and healed his servant.

Faith connects us to fellow believers and to God. At the end of Bible studies
at my church, we pair with someone to be prayer partners for the week.
Taking time to listen to someone's prayer request and then lifting their
need to the Lord is powerful. It reminds us we are not alone. Checking
in with our prayer partner during the week shows we care and reminds
them of our prayers. We realize our faith intercedes on their behalf, and
we extend the love of God to them.

*"Ever since I first heard of your strong faith in the Lord Jesus
and your love for God's people everywhere, I have not stopped
thanking God for you. I pray for you constantly."*
~ Ephesians 1:15-16 (NLT)

28

God in our Midst

"The Lord your God is in your midst, a mighty one who will save; he will rejoice over you with gladness; he will quiet you by his love; he will exult over you with loud singing."
~ Zephaniah 3:17 (ESV)

Zephaniah was a prophet who wrote a three-chapter book in the Old Testament. The book tells about the coming of the Lord, and the judgment against Judah and Jerusalem, who were in rebellion. The book also shares the importance of seeking God first.

This verse shares the hope that was extended to the remnant of Judah when they returned to the Lord. It provides the same encouragement for us, reminding us the Lord is in our midst. It shares God's response to us.

The thought, *"The Lord your God is in your midst,"* was strange to the people in Old Testament days. People viewed God as a faraway, distant God who dwelt only in the temple and tabernacle. Occasionally God would appear to someone, as He did with Moses at Mt. Sinai when He gave him the Ten Commandments.

We know from the New Testament:

"The Word became flesh and made his dwelling among us. We have seen his glory, the glory of the one and only Son, who came from the Father, full of grace and truth."
~ John 1:14

*"Through him you Gentiles are also being made part of
this dwelling where God lives by his Spirit."*
~ Ephesians 2:22 (NLT)

Indeed, God's presence is found in you and me, thanks to God sending
Jesus to live among us. Through the Holy Spirit, God truly is in our midst.

Do you live differently when you keep foremost in your mind, *"God is truly
in your midst, He is the mighty one who will save and restore you"*? During
those moments when you feel alone, turn your thoughts toward God and
know He is always with you and in you. What a difference that makes in
changing your attitude. Despite the problems in this world, you know God
cares for you and loves you. In Him, you have salvation.

When you return to the Lord, what does God do? Your Daddy (Abba)
rejoices over you with gladness. He quiets you with His love. He exults over
you with loud singing. How beautiful is that image? If you are a parent,
can you relate to that vision?

May you continually seek the Lord. Reflect on how God cares and loves
you so very much. He is always with you, rejoicing and exulting over you.
You bring a song to His voice.

*"The Lord appeared to us in the past, saying: 'I have loved you with
an everlasting love; I have drawn you with unfailing kindness.'"*
~ Jeremiah 31:3

29

The Armor of God

The temperature at a park was about 38 degrees. I put on layer after layer of coats and sweatshirts to keep warm while I sat in nature enjoying God's presence. I thought of the armor of God that we, as Christians, need to put on daily to withstand the enemy. We need to keep our eyes on the cross where victory has been achieved through Jesus' death and resurrection.

> *"Finally, be strong in the Lord and in his mighty power. Put on the full armor of God, so that you can take your stand against the devil's schemes. For our struggle is not against flesh and blood, but against the rulers, against the authorities, against the powers of this dark world and against the spiritual forces of evil in the heavenly realms. Therefore put on the full armor of God, so that when the day of evil comes, you may be able to stand your ground, and after you have done everything, to stand."*
> ~ Ephesians 6:10-13

So many of the struggles we face are against the devil; against things we cannot see.

> Do you ever think you aren't good enough and don't measure up? Do you believe you will never be successful and aren't worthy of love?

Those are lies from the enemy. We need to fight those lies and negative thoughts by putting on the full armor of God so we can stand our ground.

Let's continue looking at the subsequent verses about the armor of God.

Christine M. Fisher

"Stand firm then, with the <u>belt of truth</u> buckled around your waist…" (v. 14)

The belt of truth, the first piece of the armor, is the Word of God. As we know, Satan is the father of lies. While speaking to some Jews, Jesus said,

"You belong to your father, the devil, and you want to carry out your father's desire. He was a murderer from the beginning, not holding to the truth, for there is no truth in him. When he lies, he speaks his native language, for he is a liar and the father of lies."
~ John 8:44

"Sanctify them by the truth; your word is truth."
~ John 17:17

"So Jesus said to the Jews who had believed him, 'If you abide in my word, you are truly my disciples, and you will know the truth, and the truth will set you free.'"
~ John 8:31-32 (ESV)

We need to stay diligent in reading and meditating on the Word so that we know the truth. With the truth, we can gird our loins and fight the enemy. Speak truth into your life.

"…with the <u>breastplate of righteousness</u> in place," (v. 14)

What armor are we to put on the main part of our body? Righteousness! Righteousness is being made right with God.

"This is how we know who the children of God are and who the children of the devil are: Anyone who does not do what is right is not a child of God; nor is anyone who does not love his brother and sister."
~ 1 John 3:10

"God made him who had no sin to be sin for us,
so that in him we might become the righteousness of God."
~ 2 Corinthians 5:21

How do we live a righteous life? By following Jesus' example. He loved everyone, shared the Good News of salvation, and did what was right in God's eyes.

"…and with your feet fitted with the readiness that
comes from the gospel of peace." (v. 15)

Our feet must always be ready to go wherever needed to bring the Good News, the gospel of peace, to others.

"But the Lord said to her, 'My dear Martha, you are worried and upset
over all these details! There is only one thing worth being concerned about.
Mary has discovered it, and it will not be taken away from her.'"
~ Luke 10:41-42 (NLT)

"Because of the tender mercy of our God, whereby the sunrise shall
visit us from on high to give light to those who sit in darkness and
in the shadow of death, to guide our feet into the way of peace."
~ Luke 1:78-79 (ESV)

"Again Jesus said, 'Peace be with you! As the
Father has sent me, I am sending you.'"
~ John 20:21

We need to shake off worry and anxiety, replacing it with the anchor of peace and hope, sharing the Good News.

"In addition to all this, take up the shield of faith, with which you
can extinguish all the flaming arrows of the evil one." (v. 16)

Christine M. Fisher

Our faith can stand the test of time by fighting the evil one.

*"Be alert and of sober mind. Your enemy the devil prowls around like
a roaring lion looking for someone to devour. Resist him, standing
firm in the faith, because you know that the family of believers
throughout the world is undergoing the same kind of sufferings."*
~ 1 Peter 5:8-9

*"And it is impossible to please God without faith. Anyone
who wants to come to him must believe that God exists
and that he rewards those who sincerely seek him."*
~ Hebrews 11:6 (NLT)

*"For everyone who has been born of God overcomes the world.
And this is the victory that has overcome the world—our faith."*
~ 1 John 5:4 (ESV)

Our faith is greater than the enemy and all other obstacles. We have the
victory through Jesus. He has overcome the world.

"Take the <u>helmet of salvation</u>..." (v. 17)

One of the first steps in a relationship with Jesus is accepting the gift of
His salvation. How fitting we have the helmet of salvation.

*"If you declare with your mouth, 'Jesus is Lord,'
and believe in your heart that God raised him
from the dead, you will be saved."*
~ Romans 10:9

May we always be grateful for the gift of salvation that guides us. It is the
greatest gift we have, and we have the honor of sharing it with others.

"…and the <u>sword of the Spirit</u>, which is the Word of God." (v. 17)

"For the word of God is alive and powerful. It is sharper
than the sharpest two-edged sword, cutting between
soul and spirit, between joint and marrow.
It exposes our innermost thoughts and desires."
~ Hebrews 4:12 (NLT)

"And <u>pray in the Spirit</u> on all occasions with all kinds
of prayers and requests. With this in mind, be alert and
always keep on praying for all the saints." (v. 18)

"Devote yourselves to prayer, being watchful and thankful."
~ Colossians 4:2

If we take to heart the sword of the Spirit and praying in the Spirit, we will be able to withstand the spiritual battles that come our way. Be encouraged to consciously put on the full armor of God, piece by piece. Be ready for battle protected with the armor of God, the Word, and prayer. You are victorious because of what Christ did for you.

"Therefore, my brothers and sisters, you whom I love and long for, my
joy and crown, stand firm in the Lord in this way, dear friends!"
~ Philippians 4:1

30

Lay it Down

There are many Bible stories of how Jesus went away from the crowds to spend time alone with God, His Father. I imagine He did this multiple times daily to continually seek and carry out God's will.

Since I started going daily to a prayer garden, God has blessed me with His presence. A brick path leads to a circle with a cross in the center and three benches. I enjoy gazing at the cross and getting lost in thought and prayer.

The first day I was there, a robin promptly greeted me, singing praises to the Creator. I had just published my thoughts about birds. God, as He often does, made me smile while thinking of His goodness and presence in every detail of our lives.

Considering the brick paths that surround the cross, I thought of different parallels with our lives. The two sets of bricks laid in circles reminded me how sometimes we go in circles, avoiding God and Jesus. We should aim to get and stay close to the cross. How wonderful when we take a step closer to the cross by taking one of the four paths that lead to the center. The cross is the centrality of our faith in Jesus.

One day big raindrops started teeming down. I sought shelter on the porch of a nearby ministry house until the rain slowed. In the storms of life, we can find shelter in Jesus and at the foot of the cross. He is always with us.

Another day, the sun was shining and I soaked up the "Son's presence." I observed three birds making a lot of noise. One remained on his branch. My thoughts went to a sermon about the Trinity–Father, Son, and Holy Spirit. The bird on the branch symbolized God in my mind. One of the two remaining birds flew around and around, reminding me of the Holy Spirit, always at work in our lives. The third bird represented Jesus, our friend.

When viewing the cross and the two-step base, I thought of Mary at the foot of the cross. Although the Bible doesn't say specifically, it is easy to imagine Mary holding Jesus' limp body when He was taken from the cross. What sorrow and pain, pure agony at seeing her son dead. Yet, she knew it was God's will: Jesus was fulfilling His mission.

What burden can you lay at the foot of the cross? Laying your fear, anger, and concern about your loved ones at the foot of the cross is a beautiful and powerful thing to do and reflect upon when gazing at the cross.

What a great reminder for us to…

lay it down. Give your problems to Jesus.
talk freely with Him, expressing your innermost thoughts.
know He is always listening and always cares.

"There is no greater love than to lay down one's life for one's friends."
~ John 15:13 (NLT)

31

Seek Him

Be still and soak in God's presence in the beauty around you. When you seek Him and find Him, you have found the greatest treasure this world holds.

"You will seek me and find me when you seek me with all your heart."
~ Jeremiah 29:13

"For where your treasure is, there your heart will be also."
~ Matthew 6:21

Going to different parks on Sundays helps me take time to seek Him and find His presence in nature, in silence, and even in the sounds around me. I especially find His presence while spending time near bodies of water.

When I take road trips, it is easy to seek and find Him. How I bask in His presence as I am on the open highway. Setting the cruise control, seeing the hills of trees, desolate farm areas, the various cloud formations and the sun fills my soul with His presence. It provides time to seek and find the Lord in prayer and worship.

On a recent outing, the park had no body of water. I was pleasantly surprised to seek and find God's presence anyway. I found Him on a short hike in the woods, through some huge fields of goldenrod and grassy paths that led to an open field.

I decided to sit, read, and write my reflection at a picnic table off the path. There was a field of goldenrod on one side and an open field on the other. I found Him as I gazed upon a field with many trees at the far edge.

Christine M. Fisher

Listening to the songs of birds drowned out the sound of cars going by in the distance.

It was a little chilly, though the sun was beating down, filling my heart and soul with His warmth. It was symbolic seeing the sun high in the sky and thinking how Jesus, the Son, reigns over everything. I love to face the sun, close my eyes, and soak up the warmth, letting Him fill every pore with His presence.

Watching the wind cause the sway of the goldenrod and other flowers reminded me of the Holy Spirit's presence. It displayed more of the beauty in finding the Lord. I was lost in thought, watching the white butterflies as they, too, praised our Creator. How perfect that these verses encourage us to seek the Lord:

"And those who know your name put their trust in you, for you,
O Lord, have not forsaken those who seek you."
~ Psalm 9:10 (ESV)

"One thing I ask from the Lord, this only do I seek: that I may
dwell in the house of the Lord all the days of my life, to gaze
on the beauty of the Lord and to seek him in his temple."
~ Psalm 27:4

We, who know the Lord, can trust Him in everything.
We have the assurance that He never forsakes us.
We have the honor of dwelling in the house of the Lord all our days.
We can gaze on the beauty of the Lord all around us.

Seek Him with all your heart, and you will find Him. God is truly the greatest treasure this world has to offer.

I encourage you to seek Him...

in all you do.
in all you see.
in all you are.

"I love those who love me, and those who seek me diligently find me."
~ Proverbs 8:17 (ESV)

32

Compassion

Compassion is another important charism Jesus shared that His Father modeled for Him. We also need to follow in God's footsteps, sharing compassion in our lives.

One definition of compassion is sympathetic pity and concern for the sufferings or misfortunes of others. The word compassion, in Hebrew and Greek, includes a broader definition: "To love, showing pity and mercy." Compassion is a form of love for those who are suffering or vulnerable which leads us to take action.

THE COMPASSION OF GOD

When the Israelites realize their sin and confess.

> *"They refused to listen and failed to remember the miracles you performed among them. They became stiff-necked and in their rebellion appointed a leader in order to return to their slavery. But you are a forgiving God, gracious and compassionate, slow to anger and abounding in love. Therefore you did not desert them."*
> ~ Nehemiah 9:17

God has a heart of compassion for His people and does not want any to walk in darkness and be lost. God's compassion led Him to action. Our action is to keep His covenant promises. We should not desert those who rebel against Him, and we should remember all His people fondly with a heart that yearns to share His love.

THE COMPASSION OF JESUS

"Jesus called his disciples to him and said, 'I have compassion for these people; they have already been with me three days and have nothing to eat. I do not want to send them away hungry, or they may collapse on the way.'"
~ Matthew 15:32

Jesus lived a life of compassion in His three short years of public ministry, which led Him to action. His ministry concentrated on loving people no matter their circumstances, what they did, or failed to do. It was an unconditional, pure love we are to emulate. We are called to heal the sick, feed the hungry, and calm the storms in their lives. Consider the ultimate way Jesus showed compassion for all of humankind:

"Christ suffered for our sins once for all time. He never sinned, but he died for sinners to bring you safely home to God. He suffered physical death, but he was raised to life in the Spirit."
~ 1 Peter 3:18 (NLT)

The greatest way Jesus shared compassion and showed us such love, pity, and mercy, was by dying on the cross. He did this so we can be set free from sin and live with Him in heaven for all eternity. What a powerful action. Indeed, what a compassionate and gracious Jesus we serve.

OUR COMPASSION

"Therefore, as God's chosen people, holy and dearly loved, clothe yourselves with compassion, kindness, humility, gentleness and patience."
~ Colossians 3:12

While at a baseball game, I witnessed a man helping an elderly woman using a walker. She slowly made her way to the sidelines and sat in her chair. When the game was over, I saw the man help her leave. Seeing them

Christine M. Fisher

filled my heart with love and compassion, and I prayed for them. To help them in a small way, I folded her chair and carried it for them.

What are some ways you can show compassion?

Love and compassion go hand in hand. I encourage you to practice acts of compassion as you follow the example of Jesus. Stay alert to serve those around you. May the Spirit lead you to see different ways to lay down your life for others.

> *"Yet this I call to mind and therefore I have hope:*
> *Because of the Lord's great love we are not consumed,*
> *for his compassions never fail."*
> ~ Lamentations 3:21-22

33

The Barren Desert

Looking at the bare trees in late fall, one can sense the winter months quickly approaching. Have you ever felt like barren trees?

> Feeling like you are stripped of everything,
> nothing seems to be going right,
> the wind has been knocked out of your sails,
> the rug pulled out from under your feet?

Life can be quite difficult when we feel stripped of everything. Often we wonder why God allows certain things to happen. These times may bring us to our knees in desperation. We search for God's presence, trying to find His loving touch and embrace.

> Gazing at the sun shining so brightly on the
> barren trees made me think…
> when we are stripped of everything in this
> world, we still have everything!
> We have the most important thing, God in our
> lives. He is still shining on and in us.

I thought about the Old Testament story of Job who was blessed abundantly by God. He was blameless and an upright man. God and Satan discussed Job's character. God granted Satan permission to remove all "things" in Job's life except for his wife. All remaining family, servants, and animals died. Even Job's house collapsed. Job then experienced painful sores from the soles of his feet to the top of his head. He was in much physical and emotional agony.

Christine M. Fisher

Despite all these losses and tragedies, Job stayed persistent in his belief in God and His goodness. Even when his friends tried to convince Job his troubles came because of sin in his life, Job stayed faithful to God and His ways. God restored to Job all that had been lost. He had more children, animals, and wealth, because he fully trusted the Lord with his life and everything that happened.

Take a few minutes to reflect on some takeaways from the story of Job:

> God can use your suffering to test and strengthen you.
> God's ways are not your ways.
> God is always with you.
> God knows your pain.
> Trust God even in your suffering.
> Depend solely on the Lord.
> Continue to praise God.
> God is the one who sustains you—not the things in this world.
> God's presence in your suffering will guide and protect you.

When going through the barren desert in life, be encouraged to seek the Lord and godly counsel. Keep reaching for Him, knowing He is always with you and guiding you.

May you be able to say,

> *"Naked I came from my mother's womb, and naked I will depart.*
> *The Lord gave and the Lord has taken away;*
> *may the name of the Lord be praised."*
> ~ Job 1:21

> *"Then Job replied to the Lord:*
> *'I know that you can do all things; no purpose of yours can be thwarted.'"*
> ~ Job 42:1-2

"In an outburst of anger I turned my back on you — but only for a moment.
It's with lasting love that I'm tenderly caring for you."
~ Isaiah 54:8 (MSG)

34

Obedience

Jesus chose to model the ultimate act of obedience to God, His Father, for you and me. In the Old Testament days, the people offered burnt offerings and sacrifices to God and were bound by the Covenant of the Law. After Jesus was born, the new Covenant was one of love.

> *"But Samuel replied: 'Does the Lord delight in burnt offerings and sacrifices as much as in obeying the voice of the Lord? To obey is better than sacrifice, and to heed is better than the fat of rams.'"*
> ~ 1 Samuel 15:22

> *"And this is love: That we walk in obedience to his commands. As you have heard from the beginning, his command is that you walk in love."*
> ~ 2 John 6

Love cannot be separated from obedience. Do you sometimes find it difficult to be obedient to God?

> *"If you love me, keep my commandments."*
> ~ John 14:15

Maybe He's calling you…

> out of your comfort zone to witness to someone.
> to change your plans and try something new.
> to take a leap of faith and let go of control in an area of your life.

Are there times when you have not obeyed God? Our first parents, Adam and Eve, were the first people who disobeyed God while in the Garden of Eden.

"The Lord God took the man and put him in the Garden of Eden to work it and take care of it. And the Lord God commanded the man, 'You are free to eat from any tree in the garden; but you must not eat from the tree of the knowledge of good and evil, for when you eat from it you will surely die.'"
~ Genesis 2:15-17

The serpent questioned Eve causing her to doubt what God said.

"When the woman saw that the fruit of the tree was good for food and pleasing to the eye, and also desirable for gaining wisdom, she took some and ate it. She also gave some to her husband, who was with her, and he ate it."
~ Genesis 3:6

Adam and Eve disobeyed God, which is when sin first entered the world. Then God put into action His ultimate and redemptive plan to restore the broken relationship to Himself. God planned to send Jesus to earth, as both divine and human, to take on the sins of the world while hanging on a cross. Three days after his earthly death, Jesus arose from the grave to bring us victory over death and eternal life. Jesus restored our relationship with God, our Father.

One of the most beautiful celebrations of the Easter season is Holy Thursday. It encourages me to reflect on what Jesus did for me. It is powerful to think of Him celebrating the Last Supper with His disciples and washing their feet to show us how we, too, need to love and serve others.

When Jesus knew the time was drawing near for Him to die, He took His disciples with Him to pray and seek God in a quiet place. He was seeking God for strength to endure the cross, knowing He would suffer physically, emotionally, and spiritually. His natural man needed the strength to walk through the divine will of His Father.

> *"Father, if you are willing, take this cup from me; yet not my will, but yours be done. An angel from heaven appeared to him and strengthened him. And being in anguish, he prayed more earnestly, and his sweat was like drops of blood falling to the ground."*
> ~ Luke 22:42-44

Jesus chose to be obedient, despite knowing the agony He would have to experience. Jesus endured the temporary separation from God, His Father, when He shouldered our sins. I am thankful for the obedience of Christ.

> *"Although he was a son, Jesus learned obedience from what he suffered and, once made perfect, he became the source of eternal salvation for all who obey him."*
> ~ Hebrews 5:8-9 (ESV)

What examples of obedience did Jesus provide that Adam and Eve failed to do?

> Seeking God's will.
> Praying continually.
> Trusting God's plan.
> Choosing to obey God.

> *"Jesus replied, 'If anyone loves me, he will obey my teaching. My Father will love him, and we will come to him and make our home with him. He who does not love me will not obey my teaching. These words you hear are not my own; they belong to the Father who sent me.'"*
> ~ John 14:23-24

35

Cascading Love

My birthday one year was a quiet day of running errands, but God's presence was with me. What better place than to be alone with Him as I pondered the meaning of my life, and how God is working in and through me.

My life song is *Offering*² by Third Day. What great truth there is in this verse from the song:

> This is my offering, dear Lord
> This is my offering to you, God
> I will give you my life
> For it's all I have to give
> Because you gave your life for me.

We should live our lives each day as an offering to God, considering the sacrifice He made of His Son, Jesus. All that we do and all we are rests on that.

Our lives are the only offering we can truly give back to God by the...

> way we love Him and others.
> things we do daily.
> condition of our heart, seeking and pleasing Him.

Spending the lunch hour with my college son was a bonus. Stopping by a waterfall on my way home was an added encounter with the Lord. God's masterpieces of creation surround us, showing us the great love He has for us. An hour flew by as I soaked up the sun, listening to the roaring water and thinking about God's love. The word "cascade" came to mind as I observed the beauty. I thought of God's love and presence cascading over our lives. I wondered if the word "cascade" is mentioned in the Bible, and if so, what is the reference?

> *"Let praise cascade off my lips; after all, you've taught me the truth about life! And let your promises ring from my tongue; every order you've given is right."*
> ~ Psalm 119:171-172 (MSG)

> *"May grace and perfect peace cascade over you as you live in the rich knowledge of God and of Jesus our Lord. Everything we could ever need for life and godliness has already been deposited in us by his divine power…"*
> ~ 2 Peter 1:2-3 (TPT)

> *"From Judah, a loving servant of Jesus, the Anointed One, and brother of Jacob. I'm writing to the chosen ones who are wrapped in the love of Father God—kept and guarded for Jesus, the Messiah. May God's mercy, peace, and love cascade over you!"*
> ~ Jude 1:1-2 (TPT)

May praise cascade from our lips, just as the water continually cascades from the waterfall. God has taught us the truth of life through His word. We can stand on the promises He has given us.

May God's grace, perfect peace, mercy, and love cascade over our lives. As we grow in our knowledge of and in relationship with God, grace and perfect peace are the by-products produced. We have all we need through Jesus' divine power in our lives. We are God's chosen ones, wrapped in the Father's love because of Jesus.

There are a few verses mentioning the sound involved with cascading waters:

> *"Then I looked, and there on Mount Zion stood the Lamb, and*
> *with Him were 144,000 who had His name and His Father's name*
> *written on their foreheads. I heard a sound from heaven like the*
> *sound of cascading waters and like the rumbling of loud thunder.*
> *The sound I heard was also like harpists playing on their harps."*
> ~ Revelation 14:1-2 (HCSB)

> *"Then I heard something like the voice of a vast multitude, like the sound of*
> *cascading waters, and like the rumbling of loud thunder, saying: Hallelujah,*
> *because our Lord God, the Almighty, has begun to reign! Let us be glad,*
> *rejoice, and give Him glory, because the marriage of the Lamb has come,*
> *and His wife has prepared herself. She was given fine linen to wear, bright*
> *and pure. For the fine linen represents the righteous acts of the saints."*
> ~ Revelation 19:6-8 (HCSB)

What do we learn from these Bible verses? The sound of cascading waters can be heard in the presence of the Lamb of God in heaven. The sound is like the rumbling of loud thunder, yet it is as beautiful as harp music. What a glorious sound it will be, listening to the multitudes of people combining to give all glory and praise to God, and God alone.

Eventually the sun appeared on the waterfall, reminding me how the Son shines through our lives, touching one person after another. We reflect His beauty and warmth to one another. Getting sprinkles of the cascading water on me, though I was far away, was a reminder of the refreshment we have in spreading the Good News of Jesus daily.

The mighty force of the waters reveals how God's presence engulfs and overtakes us. What joy we experience when we discover Him in our lives.

God's great love and power continually cascade over us. Embrace that beauty. God's love is so deep and wide.

"Then Christ will make his home in your hearts as you trust in him. Your roots will grow down into God's love and keep you strong. And may you have the power to understand, as all God's people should, how wide, how long, how high, and how deep his love is. May you experience the love of Christ, though it is too great to understand fully. Then you will be made complete with all the fullness of life and power that comes from God."
~ Ephesians 3:17-19 (NLT)

36

Come, Follow Me

When Jesus called His first disciples, He was a stranger, calling them from afar. Some of them heard about Jesus from a friend or relative. Still others Jesus knew personally when He called them.

Isn't that like us? There are some who slowly realize something is missing and feel a beckoning from a stranger named Jesus. Some learn about Jesus from a friend or relative, and hear Jesus calling them to heed Him. Still others know about Jesus and realize they need a personal relationship with Him.

Many of the disciples left everything to follow Jesus. They left their mother, brother, job, and even home. Many of them immediately left what they were doing to follow Jesus. They trusted that Jesus was in charge of their lives and would provide for them no matter what.

Jesus still calls us, saying, *"Come, follow Me."*

> In what ways has Jesus called you?
> Is His call to *"Come, follow Me"* the most important thing in your life?
> Do you follow His lead daily, going where He leads?
> Have you left your family, your job or home to follow His call?
> Maybe you haven't heard the Lord's call so drastically in your life.

Christine M. Fisher

Reflecting on Jesus' call to His first disciples shows us how to follow His call…

>to place Him first.
>to follow His call daily.
>to be dependent on Him alone to provide.

>*"Jesus replied: 'Love the Lord your God with all your heart and with all your soul and with all your mind.'"*
>~ Matthew 22:37

37

Shadows

One day at my prayer garden, I saw many shadows. Some shadows were cast upon the cross, the brick wall in the distance, and even on the bricks in front of me. This made me consider "shadows" in our lives. As a youngster, I was afraid of my shadow, thinking there was some mysterious person walking with me.

I watched the progression of the shadows throughout the 45 minutes I was there. It was strange when I closed my eyes for a bit and then opened them to see no more shadows. The light was gone, signaling the end of another day in God's kingdom, gone in the blink of an eye.

I was interested to find Scripture passages about shadows to see what lessons God was showing me. The passages that spoke to my heart were those that talk about the shadow of His wings. What are our lives like as we live in the shadow of God's wings?

> *"Have mercy on me, O God, have mercy! I look to you for protection. I will hide beneath the shadow of your wings until the danger passes by."*
> ~ Psalm 57:1 (NLT)

> *"Keep me as the apple of your eye; hide me in the shadow of your wings."*
> ~ Psalm 17:8

> *"They shall return and dwell beneath my shadow; they shall flourish like the grain; they shall blossom like the vine; their fame shall be like the wine of Lebanon."*
> ~ Hosea 14:7 (ESV)

Christine M. Fisher

"Whoever dwells in the shelter of the Most High
will rest in the shadow of the Almighty."
~ Psalm 91:1

"Because you are my helper, I sing for joy in the shadow of your wings."
~ Psalm 63:7 (NLT)

These verses demonstrate how the shadow of God's wings is the place of refuge, rest, and refreshment.

A young bird instinctively seeks refuge, rest, and refreshment under the shadow of its mother's wings. We need to seek refuge, rest, and refreshment under the shadow of God's wings. He provides that in our lives as we continually dwell with Him.

In thinking about shadows, I like knowing the truth that the light, the sun needed to produce a shadow, is God Himself, the True Light. We know when we are in heaven the light will shine bright forever. There will be no darkness.

When you look and see your shadow may it be a reminder that God is walking beside you, providing refuge, rest, and refreshment, with every step. May His light shine so brightly in our lives that we cast that same shadow into the lives of everyone we meet.

"How priceless is your unfailing love, O God! People
take refuge in the shadow of your wings."
~ Psalm 36:7

38

I Have Overcome

"If the world hates you, keep in mind that it hated me first."
~ John 15:18

"These things I have spoken to you, so that in Me you may have peace. In the world you have tribulation, but take courage; I have overcome the world."
~ John 16:33 (NASB)

Have you ever felt rejected by people?

> Maybe you didn't get the job you thought would be perfect.
> Maybe you were told there wasn't a spot for you on a sports team.
> Maybe your essay wasn't good enough, which meant you couldn't be included in a special club.
> Maybe the program you wanted to participate in didn't accept you.

How do you handle the rejections that are a natural part of life?

> Do the rejections get you down?
> Do you feel God is not on your side, and that nothing works out like it should?

My youngest son says, "You control what bothers you." As I was lamenting the rejections my son was experiencing, it occurred to me that Jesus, the Son of God, was often rejected by men.

"He was in the world, and the world was made through
him, yet the world did not know him. He came to his
own, and his own people did not receive him."
~ John 1:10-11 (ESV)

Jesus left heaven and came to earth as the Messiah, and His own people, the Jews, did not believe He was the One. They rejected Him.

"He was despised and rejected by men; a man of sorrows,
and acquainted with grief; and as one from whom men hide
their faces he was despised, and we esteemed him not."
~ Isaiah 53:3 (ESV)

Jesus' life on earth was filled with sorrow when people rejected Him, not accepting the love He brought. They did not recognize Jesus as the Savior.

"The stone that the builders rejected has become the cornerstone."
~ Psalm 118:22 (ESV)

Though many in Jesus' day rejected Him, God's plan for Jesus to save us from our sins became the foundation for our faith. It all starts with Jesus.

"As you come to him, a living stone rejected by men but in the sight
of God chosen and precious, you yourselves like living stones are
being built up as a spiritual house, to be a holy priesthood, to offer
spiritual sacrifices acceptable to God through Jesus Christ."
~ 1 Peter 2:4-5 (ESV)

As we come to accept Jesus and build our foundation on Him, our faith comes alive.

"And all the people in the synagogue were filled with rage as
they heard these things; and they got up and drove Him out of
the city, and led Him to the brow of the hill on which their city

had been built, in order to throw Him down the cliff. But He
walked right through the crowd and went on His way."
~ Luke 4:28-30 (NASB)

Jesus was teaching in His hometown of Nazareth, reading the scroll of Isaiah, stating the prophecy was fulfilled through Him. They did not believe or like the things Jesus said so He walked away and moved on.

"But first he must suffer many things and be rejected by this generation."
~ Luke 17:25 (ESV)

Before the Son of Man came in all His glory, He came willingly to earth to suffer and endure the rejection of many. The greatest rejection Jesus faced was death on the cross. How did He handle rejection? By accepting the situation, taking time to pray to God, and loving everyone, even those who were inflicting the rejection upon Him. We never read stories of Jesus feeling angry for the rejections He endured.

What kept Jesus fueled when He was rejected?

Knowing…

> He belonged to God, His Father.
> what people thought of Him did not ultimately matter.
> His identity was based only on what His Father said about Him.
> God has the ultimate victory over everything.

These are also great statements to fuel us when we face rejection. Despite all the rejections Jesus experienced, most importantly, His death on a cross, He overcame. Jesus was victorious. You and I will spend eternity in Heaven because Jesus overcame rejection from men.

"I have been crucified with Christ. It is no longer
I who live, but Christ who lives in me.
And the life I now live in the flesh I live by faith in the Son of God,
who loved me and gave himself for me."
~ Galatians 2:20 (ESV)

39

The Desert Experience

"May the Christ Child be your guiding star in the desert of this present life." –Padre Pio

Our life can be considered a desert experience, a wandering in the wilderness, until we reach our true home. God has given us this desert experience to draw closer to Him, to prepare our heart to spend eternity in the Promised Land of Heaven. He provides just what we need when we need it.

I was reminded of that parallel thinking of the Israelites who wandered in the desert for 40 years. Below is synopsis of the story from Numbers 13:1-13.

God said Canaan would be the new home for the Israelites. Moses assigned 12 spies to explore the land of Canaan for 40 days. They were to report on their findings. Ten of the spies showed little faith, saying the land was gloomy, not acceptable, and would not be inhabitable. Life would be too difficult there. Only two spies, Joshua and Caleb, came back with a good, positive report saying the land was good. They knew God would work everything out.

The ten spies who gave the negative report were struck down and died of a plague. Joshua and Caleb were saved. The Israelites still believed the reports of the ten spies. God was angered that they did not want the land of Canaan, so the Israelites were made to wander in the desert, the wilderness, for 40 years.

The Israelites were tested while in the wilderness. Despite God's anger, He still revealed His glory to the people providing for their needs. They saw God's glory, His love, mercy, forgiveness, and goodness.

In the desert, God provided quail and manna for the people, providing what they needed each day. The manna would spoil if they tried to save it for the next day (Exodus 16). Moses died before entering Canaan. God chose Joshua to lead the Israelites through the Jordan River to the Promised Land.

> *"The Lord your God has blessed you in all the work of your hands. He has watched over your journey through this vast wilderness. These forty years the Lord your God has been with you, and you have not lacked anything."*
> ~ Deuteronomy 2:7

Our desert experience gives us the opportunity to build a personal relationship with God. We must first accept the fact that God exists and make Him our personal Lord and Savior. As we see God working in our lives, we grow in faith and trust of our Creator. Do you trust God more because you see His faithfulness in your life?

As we go about our life, we can continually talk to God about everything. Do you talk to Him throughout your day, asking Him to help you or share how you are feeling?

Our lives are full of choices because God granted us free will. Do you make good choices basing your decisions on God's word? Walking by faith means letting God guide our steps. Do you seek to walk with God, letting Him guide your steps? Do you take time daily to seek God's will?

God is always working in our lives, providing what we need when we need it. Do you take time to see how God faithfully provides for you, even in the little things? God is our good Father who always gives us something to be thankful for no matter how bad the situation. Try to focus on the positive in all situations, and remember God works everything out for our good if we love Him and are called according to His purposes.

God reveals His glory, His presence, every moment of every day. Do you see His glory in creation from the animals to the flowers, to every human being? Try to live in the present, not living in the past, not living in the future. Live in the present and enjoy the gift that the present is!

> "'Though the mountains be shaken and the hills be removed, yet my unfailing love for you will not be shaken nor my covenant of peace be removed,' says the Lord, who has compassion on you."
> ~ Isaiah 54:10

40

The Wind

One day at my prayer garden, the sun was shining accompanied by a gentle breeze. As time went on, darker clouds settled in, and it became windy. A few leaves began falling from the tree branches and, I would venture to say, the wind was howling.

Prior to the wind picking up speed, I enjoyed the warmth of the sun on my back, reminding me of the Son shining on me. When the wind was at full force, I was reminded of the Holy Spirit and the first Pentecost.

> *"On the day of Pentecost all the believers were meeting together in one place. Suddenly, there was a sound from heaven like the roaring of a mighty windstorm, and it filled the house where they were sitting. Then, what looked like flames or tongues of fire appeared and settled on each of them. And everyone present was filled with the Holy Spirit and began speaking in other languages, as the Holy Spirit gave them this ability."*
> ~ Acts 2:1-4 (NLT)

The next day, while at a park sitting near the water, the wind blew through bringing a passing rain shower. This combination stirred ripples across the water, with the surrounding greenery swaying back and forth. A few minutes later, the wind died down, making part of the water still and calm. The effect of the wind could be seen as ripples on the water in the distance.

Isn't the wind fascinating? You cannot physically see it, but you can see its effect on the water and trees, and you can feel it on your face.

The way the Holy Spirit descended on the believers that first Pentecost is a perfect representation – a mighty windstorm that filled them with the Spirit. Indeed, the Holy Spirit is like the wind. We cannot physically see the Spirit, but we can see His effects in our lives and in the lives of others. We are sent forth with the Holy Spirit in us to accomplish the Good News of sharing God's love and the gospel message of salvation.

Whenever you encounter "wind" in your life, be reminded of the Holy Spirit at work.

> Maybe it will be like a mighty rushing wind to remind you of the Holy Spirit's work in your life.
> Perhaps the wind will be like a storm in your life. Remember, Jesus can calm the storm at any moment.
> Maybe it will be like a gentle breeze to remind you of the peace the Spirit can fill you with.

Do not let the wind steer you from the course you are on; the running of the race with the Spirit leading you. Stay firmly planted.

> *"And this hope will not lead to disappointment. For we know how dearly God loves us, because he has given us the Holy Spirit to fill our hearts with his love."*
> ~ Romans 5:5 (NLT)

41

I Chose You

"As the Father has loved me, so have I loved you. Now remain in my love."
~ John 15:9

What a powerful statement. God's love for Jesus has been the perfect loving relationship for all eternity, from the very beginning of existence until the very end. I am not sure our finite minds can truly comprehend the great love God has for His only begotten Son, Jesus. It is immeasurable.

What a privilege to know Jesus loves us with the very same love God has for Him.

> Do you get a glimpse of Jesus' love when you see the beauty of nature?
> Or when the right people are in your path when you need encouragement?
> How about when a need is met unexpectedly which you did not voice to anyone?

GOD IS ALWAYS WITH JESUS; THEY ARE REALLY ONE

"Believe me when I say that I am in the Father and the Father is in me; or at least believe on the evidence of the miracles themselves."
~ John 14:11

GOD PLACED EVERYTHING IN JESUS' HANDS

"The Father loves the Son and has placed everything in his hands."
~ John 3:35

GOD LOVES JESUS, AS HE WAS THE PERFECT EXAMPLE OF OBEDIENCE SENT TO REDEEM US

"The reason my Father loves me is that I lay down
my life—only to take it up again."
~ John 10:17

GOD CALLS JESUS HIS BELOVED

"...This is my beloved Son, with whom I am well pleased; listen to him."
~ Matthew 17:5 (ESV)

We often find it difficult to understand or accept the love Jesus has for us because our human view of love is more defined and conditional. Jesus' love for us is great. He sacrificed His very life to show His great love for us. I pray this statement makes its way directly to your heart, even though your finite mind might not comprehend how someone can love you so unconditionally!

Can you imagine when we get to heaven, Jesus greeting us with "Welcome, my beloved child"?

"I no longer call you servants, because a servant does not know his
master's business. Instead, I have called you friends, for everything
that I learned from my Father I have made known to you."
~ John 15:15

Are you in awe of hearing Jesus call you "friend"? Jesus came to share with us everything He learned from God. That makes us His true friend. How fortunate we get to know everything about the Father that Jesus knows. We get to know how the story fits together. We can be assured Jesus picked us to be His friend. He is a friend who never leaves or forsakes us, and always loves us. Truly, He is the ultimate friend.

I pray you know deep in your soul that Jesus is the best friend you can ever have. What a wonderful calling to be a friend of Jesus in your lifetime.

"You did not choose me, but I chose you and appointed
you to go and bear fruit—fruit that will last..."
~ John 15:16

Jesus chose you because of His great love for you. God gave us free will in our lives to choose. Unfortunately, people don't always choose to let Jesus into their heart and change their lives forever. The privilege you have, since Jesus chose you, is to go and bear fruit that will last for all eternity!

The fruit of...

loving God above all.

joy in living out your personal relationship with God each day, knowing you are fulfilling His will.

peace which abides deep in your heart knowing God is always with you, guiding your every step.

patience with your shortcomings and with the people in your life.

kindness in the way you deal with all the different personalities and temperaments of people.

goodness with showing a mixture of righteousness and love for others.

faithfulness in standing up for what you know is God's will and nature.

gentleness with how you deal with God's creation.

self-control in dealing with impulses of the flesh which tempt you.

I pray you are filled with joy as you reflect on the fact that Jesus chose you, and you are called to bear His fruit daily. Remain in the love of Jesus and remember you are His chosen friend, chosen to know Him and to bear His fruit.

"I have made you known to them, and will continue to make you known in order that the love you have for me may be in them and that I myself may be in them."
~ John 17:26

42

The Gift of Sight

Imagine living with Jesus during His three years of public ministry. Visualize yourself as the main character in this story.

You are blind. One day, sitting on the side of the road, you hear the noise and footsteps of an excited crowd walking by.

You ask those nearby, "What is happening?"

They say, "Jesus of Nazareth is passing by."

You call out, "Jesus, Son of David, have mercy on me!"

Many in the crowd who are leading you tell you to be quiet. However, such joy and excitement arise within you that you shout even more, "Son of David, have mercy on me!"

Suddenly, Jesus stops and orders the people to bring you to Him. Jesus asks, "What do you want me to do for you?" "Lord, I want to see," you reply.

Jesus says, "Receive your sight; your faith has healed you."

Because of your faith in Him, Jesus restores your sight, and you immediately see clearly. You follow Jesus as you praise God. When those in the crowd see the miracle, they also start praising God (Luke 18:35-43).

In comparison to the story of the blind man, can you say the following are true in your life?

You have heard about Jesus of Nazareth. But…

> do you truly know Him?
>
> does He fill the void in your heart, or are you still chasing after worldly things to fill it?
>
> do you believe Jesus is the Son of David, the one who shows mercy?
>
> do you know, without a doubt, He is the true King?
>
> do you know the "Son of David" was a Messianic title, which meant He is the long-awaited Deliverer, the fulfillment of Old Testament scriptures?
>
> have you experienced the richness of His mercy in your daily life?
>
> do you have "fire in your bones" like the blind man?
>
> is the excitement and joy you experience in knowing Jesus so strong you can't help but share Him with others?
>
> is it so deep within you that nothing can stop you from sharing His love?

Do you know the depth of Jesus' great love and care for you?

> Jesus loves you personally. He takes the time to stop and show His care and concern whenever you cry out to Him.

Do you hear Jesus ask what He can do for you?

> He wants to know the deep recesses and desires of your heart. What can He do for you? Share it with Jesus. How much faith do you have in Jesus? Your faith in Jesus, believing in what we cannot always see, is what Jesus can use to heal you.

Do you see how Jesus responds to your requests?

> Even if you don't get the specific answer you want, do you experience His peace, mercy, and love when you call out to Him? Jesus will always lead you to what is best.

Christine M. Fisher

Do you follow Jesus, praising God as you go about your day?

Does praising God encourage you to follow Jesus and realize the depth of His love and graciousness in your life?

May you be encouraged to live more like that blind man…

calling out to Jesus for His mercy.
sharing with Jesus what you want Him to do for you.
sharing your heart's desire with Jesus.
looking for the miracles in your life.
following Jesus and praising God for His goodness.
sharing the excitement and joy of Jesus with all you meet.

May your heart's desire be to see Jesus with the eyes of your heart in every moment.

"That is what the Scriptures mean when they say, 'No eye has seen, no ear has heard, and no mind has imagined what God has prepared for those who love him.'"
~ 1 Corinthians 2:9 (NLT)

43

Remain in Me

In the Old Testament, Israel is referred to as a vine or vineyard and, usually, portrayed as lacking in faithfulness to God. The best vines are the ones that produce the most abundant fruit, which in turn makes the finest wine.

"I am the true vine, and my Father is the gardener."
~ John 15:1

In the New Testament, Jesus became the true vine. He is genuine, the true One, the Savior of the world. God is the Master Gardener who cares deeply for His vineyard (you and me). Jesus always points directly to God, His Father, and our Father.

"Remain in me, and I will remain in you..."
~ John 15:4 (NLT)

What a great promise Jesus shares with us. What love He has for us. He is forever with and in us. When we feel alone, when we feel Jesus is not with us, we need to say, "Jesus, I know you are with me. Come along as I walk in nature" (or whatever task you are doing). Or say, "Jesus, help me not worry about something that might happen. I know you are with me through it all." This helps refocus your thoughts with Jesus.

"I am the vine; you are the branches.
If a man remains in me and I in him, he will bear much fruit..."
~ John 15:5

As branches, we are off shoots from the vine, the source of eternal life. If we stay connected to the vine, there is abundant life to sustain us daily.

Christine M. Fisher

Did you notice how Jesus says, *"remain in me,"* in two consecutive verses? He wants our focus on the importance of that promise. Fruit is produced by staying in union and fellowship with Jesus. Our lives will bear much fruit because we are growing from the true vine.

> *"This is to my Father's glory, that you bear much*
> *fruit, showing yourselves to be my disciples."*
> ~ John 15:8

The Father, God, the Gardner, is glorified when our lives bear His fruit. Our bearing of fruit proves we are true disciples of Jesus. What is the fruit our lives bear?

> *"But the fruit of the Spirit is love, joy, peace, forbearance, kindness, goodness,*
> *faithfulness, gentleness and self-control. Against such things there is no law."*
> ~ Galatians 5:22-23

In thinking about the vine and the wine symbolism, consider the story of the first miracle of Jesus in John 2:1-11.

> *"When the wine was gone, Jesus' mother said*
> *to him, 'They have no more wine.'"*
> ~ John 2:3

In this statement, Jesus turned the water into wine for a wedding feast at Cana. Jesus' life, just like in the making of wine, was plucked away, pressed down to the point of death in a wine press. Jesus became the true vine as He prepared for His death, sharing the Last Supper with His disciples.

> *"And he took bread, gave thanks and broke it, and gave it to them,*
> *saying, 'This is my body given for you; do this in remembrance of me.'*
> *In the same way, after the supper he took the cup, saying, 'This cup*
> *is the new covenant in my blood, which is poured out for you.'"*
> ~ Luke 22:19-20

Remember, the Holy Spirit fills you and is always with you. Be encouraged to share the fruit of the Spirit with others. If you feel Jesus is not with you, practice the presence of His Spirit. Speak to Jesus, inviting Him along every step and activity you participate in. His promise is to remain with you.

"I in them and you in me, that they may become perfectly one, so that the world may know that you sent me and loved them even as you loved me."
~ John 17:23 (ESV)

Christine M. Fisher

44

God is Always at Work

One winter I observed a lake frozen with inches of ice. As I approached the lake, I was surprised to see a waterfall beneath a small bridge, flowing fresh and full of life. Under the ice, the lake world was active and alive even though it was not visible. Who would have thought there would be a waterfall when the temperature was below freezing?

I was reminded how God is always at work in every aspect of our lives. Our life journey can sometimes be like wandering in the desert or in the dark night of winter. Whatever we are walking through, even when we do not see or feel Him, He is still present and working on our behalf.

"But Jesus replied, 'My Father is always working, and so am I.'"
~ John 5:17 (NLT)

This verse shows the compassion of Jesus in healing people on the Sabbath. He shows us how the law of love is greater than the law of Moses. No matter the day or hour, God never stops working in our lives.

"And we know that in all things God works for the good of those
who love him, who have been called according to his purpose."
~ Romans 8:28

When our human eyes see only despair, we can have confidence that, if we stay grounded in Him, God is working everything out for our good. He is our sovereign Lord.

*"And I am certain that God, who began the good work
within you, will continue his work until it is finally
finished on the day when Christ Jesus returns."*
~ Philippians 1:6 (NLT)

God began a good work in us when we came to salvation in Christ. How wonderful to know He is faithful to continue this work until Jesus comes again to fulfill His kingdom on earth as in heaven.

"Indeed, he who watches over Israel never slumbers or sleeps."
~ Psalm 121:4 (NLT)

What great comfort we have in knowing God never sleeps. He never misses anything that happens in our lives.

Try to pinpoint ways you see God's presence and Him working in your life, even in the most difficult of circumstances. He is always working in you, through you, and on your behalf. He loves you with the greatest of love and wants the best for you.

*"And so we know and rely on the love God has for us. God is love.
Whoever lives in love lives in God, and God in them."*
~ 1 John 4:16

45

Temple of the Holy Spirit

"Do you not know that you are God's temple
and that God's Spirit dwells in you?"
~ 1 Corinthians 3:16 (ESV)

"Don't you realize that your body is the temple of the Holy Spirit, who lives
in you and was given to you by God? You do not belong to yourself, for God
bought you with a high price. So you must honor God with your body."
~ 1 Corinthians 6:19-20 (NLT)

"And what union can there be between God's temple and idols? For we
are the temple of the living God. As God said: 'I will live in them and
walk among them. I will be their God, and they will be my people...'"
~ 2 Corinthians 6:16 (NLT)

In the Old Testament, the temple represented a physical building that...

> contained God's presence.
> was a place of worship.
> was a place of sacrifice.

Only the high priest had access to God in the temple. The inner curtain in the temple separated the Holy Place from the Most Holy Place. The High Priest could go there once a year, on the Day of Atonement, to offer sacrifices for people's sins. When Jesus died on the cross, He became the atonement for our sin, once and for all, which forever changed the way the Old Testament temple was viewed.

*"And Jesus cried out again with a loud voice and yielded up his
spirit. And behold, the curtain of the temple was torn in two, from
top to bottom. And the earth shook, and the rocks were split."*
~ Matthew 27:50-51 (ESV)

The torn curtain signifies that Jesus has given all people the ability to come into God's presence without the barrier of sin. The temple was transformed because of Jesus' sacrifice on the cross. All believers have direct access to the temple, to God's presence, not just near us, but in us, because of the Holy Spirit. We are now the living temple!

Our body is the physical temple that...

contains God's presence.

*"No one has ever seen God. But if we love each other,
God lives in us, and his love is brought to full expression in us."*
~ 1 John 4:12 (NLT)

God's presence is in you. Let that truth sink into your heart. God is love, and we are made in His image. Once we accept Jesus into our heart, God's presence dwells in us. This love is the goodness we share with others. Our heart shares God's love.

is a place of worship.

*"Through Jesus, therefore, let us continually offer to God a sacrifice
of praise—the fruit of lips that openly profess his name."*
~ Hebrews 13:15

The simple thought of thanking God for the sunshine, the rain, and the people He puts in your path is a form of worship. Continually seeing God at work orchestrating each event with His perfect timing is worship.

Listening to music that inspires your faith journey and offering a prayer for someone who comes into your mind are also forms of worship.

is a place of sacrifice.

"Therefore, I urge you, brothers and sisters, in view of God's mercy, to offer your bodies as a living sacrifice, holy and pleasing to God—this is your true and proper worship."
~ Romans 12:1

Offering your daily struggles to the Lord, letting Him work through our circumstances, and holding onto Him are ways to be a living sacrifice to God. Do you try to accept these things with a positive attitude, despite the hardships you endure?

Since our bodies are the temple of the Holy Spirit, of God's presence, we need to consider how we treat our physical bodies, which are a gift from God. Our bodies should be treated with respect, reverence, and holiness.

Are you using your body to glorify God, or are you abusing your temple?
Are you eating properly, getting enough exercise and sleep?
Are you keeping free from addictions?
Are you focusing your thoughts on God and being an encouragement to others?

Let all you are, all you do, and all you think, be a reflection of the temple you represent as you glorify God with your life.

"We prove ourselves by our purity, our understanding, our patience, our kindness, by the Holy Spirit within us, and by our sincere love."
~ 2 Corinthians 6:6 (NLT)

46

God's Agape Love

What ways do you experience God's rich love?

How has God revealed His great love for you?

How has experiencing God's love changed you?

"Then Christ will make his home in your hearts as you trust in him. Your roots will grow down into God's love and keep you strong. And may you have the power to understand, as all God's people should, how wide, how long, how high, and how deep his love is. May you experience the love of Christ, though it is too great to understand fully. Then you will be made complete with all the fullness of life and power that comes from God."
~ Ephesians 3:17-19 (NLT)

We have the assurance that Christ is in our heart, as we trust Him more and more. Our heart, rooted in God's deep love, makes us stronger and stronger. We need His power to truly grasp the width, length, height, and depth of His love for us personally. In Paul's letter to the Ephesians, he prays we may experience Christ's love, though we cannot fully understand it in our humanness. We are made complete with the life and power, which God gives us.

"All who declare that Jesus is the Son of God have God living in them, and they live in God. We know how much God loves us, and we have put our trust in his love. God is love, and all who live in love live in God, and God lives in them. And as we live in God, our love grows more perfect. So we will not be afraid on the day of judgment, but we can face him with confidence because we live like Jesus here in this world."
~ 1 John 4:15-17 (NLT)

Christine M. Fisher

Only one word is needed to describe God. Love. In this context it refers to agape love, which is sacrificial, undeserved, not self-serving, and unconditional. God modeled agape love when He sent His only Son, Jesus, to save us from our sins so we can spend eternity with Him. God's love, mercy, and grace take the place of our sins.

It is good to know that when we put our faith in Jesus, God lives in us, and we live in Him. We then experience God's love deep in our heart, and we trust in His love in our lives. Because God lives in us, we share and grow in that same agape love. We can put others before ourselves, show unconditional love to them, and sacrifice without expecting anything in return.

One mid-December day while walking and talking with the Lord, I saw a pink cloud shaped like a heart. The next day, I saw a heart shaped in the mud. Now I see hearts all along my path. One day I saw 18 of them! God makes me smile every time.

What are some ways you experience God's love?

When I take time to walk, pray, and spend time with the Lord, I experience His love. One day He showed me shadows in the shape of crosses on a nearby brick wall. I see His love in nature when a squirrel comes near, or in a group of three birds flying by, or in beautiful sunsets. The hearts He puts in my path remind me of His heart filled with agape love for me.

How has God revealed His great love in your life?

Seeing hearts reveals God's love for me. I sense His presence knowing only He can orchestrate hearts appearing everywhere I go. I have seen them in nature and around my house. I have seen them in the sink, in my food, and on the carpet through a piece of paper that is somehow heart shaped.

Seeing the hearts makes me not only feel God's agape love personally, but I have experienced a growth of love in my heart. A heart to love others more, modeling agape love, being more understanding, and being more Christ-like. God is filling me with this love, and I am asking Him to show me what to do with it. I love myself more, knowing God's love for me is unconditional and abundant, no matter what.

How have you changed through experiencing God's love?

Christine M. Fisher

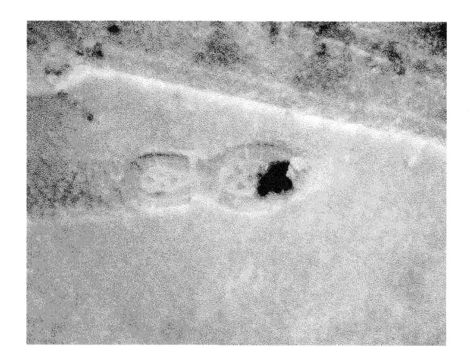

One winter day I went to my garden to sit in front of the cross. As I turned to leave, I saw my boot print with a heart shape in the snow. The next morning I checked the bottom of my boot. There is no heart design on it. I have no explanation how the heart got there. My first thought was "walking in love," and then "walking in love to the cross." That is exactly what Jesus did for us, modeling His great agape love for us.

This reminded me…

> we never walk alone; God is always with us.
> sometimes God's love carries us.

Daily seeing signs of His love through the gift of hearts, slowly I am grasping more of the width, depth, length, and height of God's agape love. It is overwhelming at times to truly understand. God is love, and I am grateful to be growing in agape love because of Him.

Look for the ways He is revealing His love and presence to you. Let His agape love change you to be more like Him.

> *"This is real love—not that we loved God, but that he loved us and sent his Son as a sacrifice to take away our sins."*
> ~ 1 John 4:10 (NLT)

Christine M. Fisher

Section 3

GOD'S LOVE ILLUMINATED IN ORDINARY LIFE

"Let all that you do be done in love."
~ 1 Corinthians 16:14 (ESV)

We can experience God's love illuminated in the ordinary moments of everyday life. It is powerful to look around and see His love revealed to us in different ways. God graces us with His love even in the humdrum moments.

Paul encourages us that all we do should be done with this love. We have the honor of living and walking in love moment by moment. We model the agape love we have been shown by God and with our lives share that love in all we do.

God's love illuminated in ordinary life.

47

A Purposeful Life

Is your purpose in this life about...

> being the most popular student in school?
> having the most trophies for a sport?
> going to the most prestigious college?
> being involved in activities to fill your time?
> wearing designer clothes?
> driving an expensive car?
> making lots of money?

Some people may say "Yes" to one or more of these questions, but that is not how I see it. I propose the purpose of our lives is about reflecting the image of God to everyone, and glorifying God in all we do and say. Our days are about spending time with God, which is the beginning of eternity, right here and now.

Is your identity found in...

> your job?
> whether you are single or married?
> whether you have children?

Some people may say "Yes" to one or more of these questions, but that is not how I see it. I propose our identity is about being a child of the King. We know Jesus died for us, and realize God sees us as perfect because of Jesus.

Is your calling limited to…

being a spouse, parent, or single person?
having a prestigious career?
taking care of a family?

Some people may say "Yes" to these questions, but that is not how I see it. I propose our calling is about using the unique gifts God has given us. We further God's kingdom by the way we live, and by sharing good works because of His love.

In every season live a purposeful life.
Live each day on purpose, with purpose,
knowing your true identity,
sharing God's calling on your life.

"The Lord will fulfill his purpose for me; your
steadfast love, O Lord, endures forever.
Do not forsake the work of your hands."
~ Psalm 138:8 (ESV)

48

Praises

God created all things to continually praise and glorify Him. We should live to praise Him through all that happens, even in the bad times and when things don't go according to our plans.

> *"You (God) love everything that exists; You do not despise anything that You have made. If You had not liked it, You would not have made it in the first place. How could anything last, if You did not want it to? How could it endure, if You had not created it? You have allowed it all to exist, O Lord, because it is Yours, and You love every living thing."*
> ~ Book of Wisdom 11:24-26

Look around. What do you see? If we agree the Lord God made everything we see, we know it remains because He wills it.

> Why do the stars appear every night?
> Why, in the fall, do the leaves turn colors and fall to the ground?
> Why do geese fly south, and the clouds bring snow in the winter?

It is because the Lord wills it and calls it forth. All creation gives praise to the Creator by fulfilling the Lord's purpose for them.

Turn your thoughts to mankind, God's greatest creation made in His image. I like this story highlighting a man who was ready to give praise to Jesus.

> *"When Jesus reached the spot, he looked up and said to him, 'Zacchaeus, come down immediately. I must stay at your house today.' So he came down at once and welcomed him gladly. Jesus said to him, 'Today*

salvation has come to this house, because this man, too, is a son of Abraham. For the Son of Man came to seek and to save the lost."
~ Luke 19:5-6, 9-10

Zacchaeus, hearing Jesus was passing by, climbed a sycamore tree because he was too short to see amidst the crowd. Jesus knew Zacchaeus' heart, that he was ready to praise his Creator, and actively sought him. What a great visit that must have been. From that point on, Zacchaeus served the Lord with joy and praise.

God gave each of us free will. It is something the rest of creation does not have. Jesus waits patiently for all His children to come to Him and praise Him with their lives. As humans, we often find it harder to praise the Lord during difficult times, especially when suffering with sickness and death.

I challenge you to continually praise and give glory to God. Yes, during the difficult times too. God is our sovereign Lord, and all creation was made to give praise and glory to Him.

"I bow before your holy Temple as I worship. I praise your name for your unfailing love and faithfulness; for your promises are backed by all the honor of your name."
~ Psalm 138:2 (NLT)

Christine M. Fisher

49

Interruptions are Opportunities

We are often so focused on tasks that interruptions seem like obstacles to accomplishing our agenda. I have a challenge for us. Let's try to look at interruptions as opportunities to communicate God's love to others, following the example of Jesus.

> *"People were bringing little children to Jesus for him to place his hands on them, but the disciples rebuked them. When Jesus saw this, He was indignant. He said to them, 'Let the little children come to me, and do not hinder them, for the kingdom of God belongs to such as these. Truly, I tell you, anyone who will not receive the kingdom of God like a little child will never enter it.' And He took the children in his arms, placed his hands on them and blessed them."*
> ~ Mark 10:13-16

Jesus did not mind being interrupted to welcome the little children into His arms. The disciples were quite surprised. Jesus showed them how important the little children are in the kingdom of God.

> *"Jesus left that place and went to the vicinity of Tyre. He entered a house and did not want anyone to know it; yet he could not keep his presence a secret. In fact, as soon as she heard about him, a woman whose little daughter was possessed by an impure spirit came and fell at his feet. The woman was a Greek, born in Syrian Phoenicia. She begged Jesus to drive the demon out of her daughter. 'First let the children eat all they want,' he told her, 'for it is not right to take the children's bread and toss it to the dogs.' 'Lord,' she replied, 'even the dogs under the table eat the children's crumbs.' Then he*

told her, 'For such a reply, you may go; the demon has left your daughter.'
She went home and found her child lying on the bed, and the demon gone."
~ Mark 7:24-30

Jesus wanted to be alone with God, but allowed for interruptions, modeling how important people are. Isn't it interesting to note the two-point message Jesus shared? When Jesus refers to "the children," He is saying that the gospel, the Good News, was to be first preached to the Jews, then the Gentiles. The woman, in faith, clearly understood what Jesus was saying. He rewarded her faith by healing her child.

"When Jesus had again crossed over by boat to the other side of the lake, a large crowd gathered around him while he was by the lake. Then one of the synagogue leaders, named Jairus, came, and when he saw Jesus, he fell at his feet. He pleaded earnestly with him, 'My little daughter is dying. Please come and put your hands on her so that she will be healed and live.' So Jesus went with him. A large crowd followed and pressed around him. And a woman was there who had been subject to bleeding for twelve years."

"...When she heard about Jesus, she came up behind him in the crowd and touched his cloak, because she thought, 'If I just touch his clothes, I will be healed.' Immediately her bleeding stopped and she felt in her body that she was freed from her suffering. At once Jesus realized that power had gone out from him. He turned around in the crowd and asked, 'Who touched my clothes?' 'You see the people crowding against you,' his disciples answered, 'and yet you can ask, "Who touched me?"' But Jesus kept looking around to see who had done it. Then the woman, knowing what had happened to her, came and fell at his feet and, trembling with fear, told him the whole truth. He said to her, 'Daughter, your faith has healed you. Go in peace and be freed from your suffering.' While Jesus was still speaking, some people came from the house of Jairus, the synagogue leader. 'Your daughter is dead,' they said. 'Why bother the teacher anymore?' Overhearing what they said, Jesus told him, 'Don't be afraid; just believe.'"

Christine M. Fisher

"After he put them all out, he took the child's father and mother and the disciples who were with him, and went in where the child was. He took her by the hand and said to her, 'Talitha koum!' (which means 'Little girl, I say to you, get up!'). Immediately the girl stood up and began to walk around (she was twelve years old)."
~ Mark 5:21-42 (Selected verses)

Jesus, on His way to help Jairus, allowed Himself to be interrupted when He stopped to see who touched His clothes. He knew immediately that healing power had left His body. He took time to acknowledge the woman because of His love for her.

In these examples, Jesus shows us that interruptions…

> are a normal part of life.
> are not something to get stressed about.
> are part of a bigger plan.
> are opportunities to further the kingdom of God.
> display God's love and power.

We can look at interruptions as opportunities to communicate God's love to another person and to experience God's love in our own life.

One winter day, I was on a tight schedule. As I was driving down our road, I noticed an elderly lady shoveling snow. Our eyes met and I could see her look of desperation. God prompted me to turn around, go back home and get my son and two shovels. We shoveled the driveway and around her mailbox. She was so appreciative. I was not able to complete my errands that day. I knew it was more important to focus on the person God put in my path and share His love with her.

Reflect on what you perceive as interruptions and allow God to use these opportunities to share and receive His love and power.

"Let no debt remain outstanding, except the continuing debt to love one another, for whoever loves others has fulfilled the law."
~ Romans 13:8

50

Through His Eyes

As Christians, our goal should be to live each day as Jesus would, seeing the world through His eyes. He cares most about how much we love Him and try to follow in His footsteps.

What would Jesus do if He were in our footsteps? How does He look at our life through His eyes and through the lens of what's most important to Him?

"Jesus replied: 'Love the Lord your God with all your heart and with all your soul and with all your mind. This is the first and greatest commandment.'"
~ Matthew 22:37-38

Through His eyes, our heart is more important than our successes or failures. He doesn't keep track of how good or bad we are at doing things. He doesn't dwell on our failures. He sees the beauty that exists within our heart.

"But the Lord said to Samuel, 'Do not consider his appearance or his height, for I have rejected him. The Lord does not look at the things people look at. People look at the outward appearance, but the Lord looks at the heart.'"
~ 1 Samuel 16:7

Through His eyes, there is no worry or fear. With Jesus, we know He will work out every detail. He says we can overcome worry or fear by trusting in Him.

"For I am the Lord, your God, who takes hold
of your right hand and says to you,
Do not fear; I will help you."
~ Isaiah 41:13

Through His eyes, there is no problem too big or that cannot be resolved. Jesus has a solution for every problem we may face. We usually want the easy way out of any problem or situation. That may not be the best solution for every situation. However, we can be assured He sees that all things work out for the good of those who love Him.

"And we know that in all things God works
for the good of those who love him,
who have been called according to his purpose."
~ Romans 8:28

Try focusing on the things Jesus sees. You will then be following in His footsteps and seeing the world through His eyes.

"The Lord opens the eyes of the blind. The Lord lifts up those
who are weighed down. The Lord loves the godly. The Lord
protects the foreigners among us. He cares for the orphans
and widows, but he frustrates the plans of the wicked."
~ Psalm 146:8-9 (NLT)

51

The Presence of the Lord

In the Old Testament, the Israelites were given the Ark of the Covenant, which contained the Ten Commandments written on two stone tablets, Aaron's rod, and manna from the wilderness. The Ark is where God would occasionally meet with specific people and was a tangible sign of His dwelling in their midst. These meetings were manifestations of God's glory to the people. Sometimes the Israelites were commanded to carry the Ark of the Covenant in front of the people. Other times they were to carry it behind them. It served as a reminder that God was always with them, guiding, protecting, and helping them every step of the way.

When God sent Jesus to earth to redeem mankind from the bondage and slavery of sin, Jesus became the new Ark of the Covenant. This is the covenant of love and grace. Jesus reveals who God is, and how He wants us to live. After Jesus died on the cross and was resurrected, God sent the Holy Spirit as our Comforter and Guide. The Holy Spirit is given to everyone who calls on the name of Jesus as Lord and Savior. Through faith, His presence is always manifested in us!

What an honor and privilege to have the presence of the Lord around us, among us, and within us.

We see evidence of the Lord's presence around us in the...

> sun, moon, stars, and clouds that fill the sky.
> mighty, majestic mountains.
> rolling plains.
> ocean waters constantly ebbing and flowing.
> awesome rock formations.

Do you see the presence of the Lord in these sights?

Take time to praise Him for the beauty He has created.

We see evidence of the Lord's presence among us in the...

person willing to lend a hand to help with a project.

ministers who encourage our relationship with the Lord to become stronger.

person who lets us know they are praying in our time of need.

community group who helped clean up from a natural disaster.

person who stopped to help when we were stranded by the side of the road.

Do you see the presence of the Lord in each of those people?

Thank the Lord for revealing His glory through them.

We see evidence of the Lord's presence within us when we...

love others unconditionally with the same love God has bestowed on us.

speak encouraging and kind words, rather than hurtful or sarcastic words.

overlook what we consider faults or shortcomings in others.

are open-minded with others, trying not to judge.

take time to listen and empathize with others going through difficult times.

We could not do these things if it were not for the grace of the Lord within us.

Ask Him to help you continue to share His presence with everyone.

"Give thanks to the Lord, for he is good. His love endures forever. Who spread out the earth upon the waters, His love endures forever. Who

made the great lights—His love endures forever. He remembered us in our
low estate His love endures forever. And freed us from our enemies. His
love endures forever. He gives food to every creature. His love endures
forever. Give thanks to the God of heaven. His love endures forever."
~ Psalm 136:1, 6-7, 23-26

52

One Week or One Weak

Imagine a week without God in our lives.
That week might look something like this:

SINDAY — A day of temptation to fall into sin more easily, not knowing right from wrong or good from evil.

MOURNDAY — A day to mourn because we missed the moments, the opportunities, to spread God's love to others.

TEARSDAY — A day of tears, not knowing how much God loves us. He is always with us and available to us.

WASTEDAY — A day wasted by not furthering the kingdom of God.

THIRSTDAY — A day of unquenchable thirst because we missed the Lord's presence and His righteousness.

FIGHTDAY — A day of fighting, unable to withstand the enemy's attacks.

SHATTERDAY — A day when everything we try to do shatters and falls apart because we are not whole.

Seven days without God makes one weak.

On the contrary, imagine a week with God in our lives.
Walking with God for one week can look more like this:

SUNDAY   We are better able to flee from sin, with the "Son" dwelling in us.

"Submit yourselves therefore to God. Resist the
devil, and he will flee from you."
~ James 4:7 (ESV)

MONDAY   Our mourning turns to dancing and joy because God is with us.

"You have turned my mourning into joyful dancing.
You have taken away my clothes of mourning and clothed me with joy."
~ Psalm 30:11 (NLT)

TUESDAY   Our tears are tears of joy!

"Tears of joy will stream down their faces, and I
will lead them home with great care.
They will walk beside quiet streams and on smooth
paths where they will not stumble.
For I am Israel's father, and Ephraim is my oldest child."
~ Jeremiah 31:9 (NLT)

WEDNESDAY   Our day is not wasted. We are fruitful, fulfilling God's plan and purpose!

"Many are the plans in a person's heart, but it
is the Lord's purpose that prevails."
~ Proverbs 19:21

"Then the way you live will always honor and please the Lord,
and your lives will produce every kind of good fruit. All the while,
you will grow as you learn to know God better and better."
~ Colossians 1:10 (NLT)

THURSDAY   Instead of an unquenchable thirst, Jesus satisfies our
             thirst with His living water, His righteousness!

"Jesus replied, 'Anyone who drinks this water will soon become thirsty again.
But those who drink the water I give will never be thirsty again.
It becomes a fresh, bubbling spring within them, giving them eternal life.'"
~ John 4:13-14 (NLT)

"Blessed are those who hunger and thirst for
righteousness, for they will be filled."
~ Matthew 5:6

FRIDAY   Putting on God's armor is the only way to fight our
             daily battles. We will be victorious with Him!

"Finally, be strong in the Lord and in the strength of his
might. Put on the whole armor of God, that you may be
able to stand against the schemes of the devil."
~ Ephesians 6:10-11 (ESV)

SATURDAY   We are made whole with God – body, mind, and spirit
             are one with Him!

"Now may the God of peace make you holy in every way,
and may your whole spirit and soul and body be kept blameless
until our Lord Jesus Christ comes again."
~ 1 Thessalonians 5:23 (NLT)

Do not be WEAK but be encouraged each WEEK to walk with the Lord
knowing He is with us and in us, every day, every moment!

Walk with Him…
one day at a time.
one week at a time.
one month at a time.
Keep your eyes and mind on Him!

"Therefore be imitators of God, as beloved children. And walk in love, as Christ loved us and gave himself up for us, a fragrant offering and sacrifice to God."
~ Ephesians 5:1-2 (ESV)

53

Thanksgiving

The word thanksgiving can be viewed as two smaller words, "thanks" and "giving," which I believe are the crux of Christian living. May our lives be full of thanks and giving.

One morning I was the recipient of a "pay it forward" at a drive-thru window. I was caught off guard and not quick enough to pass it to the car behind me. Later that day, I was at the grocery store and felt inclined to "pay it forward" with an elderly gentleman behind me in the check-out line. He was confused and didn't understand what happened. I left the store, allowing the cashier to explain it to him again.

When he walked outside the store, he saw me and said, "I'm still in shock. No one has ever done that for me." We exchanged a hug and a Happy Thanksgiving greeting. The ripple effect of one little action always amazes and blesses me. I would not have thought about blessing that man had it not been for the kindness extended to me earlier that morning.

Cambridge Dictionary's online definition of the word thanksgiving includes: "The act of saying or showing you are grateful, especially to God." I was surprised to see the "especially to God" reference in the definition.

I have included Bible verses that mention "thanksgiving" to show the implications of the word in our daily living. See if you notice anything in regard to the words "thanks" and "giving."

"I will praise God's name in song and glorify him with thanksgiving."
~ Psalm 69:30

Christine M. Fisher

"All of this is for your benefit. And as God's grace reaches more and more people, there will be great thanksgiving, and God will receive more and more glory."
~ 2 Corinthians 4:15 (NLT)

"Let us come into his presence with thanksgiving; let us make a joyful noise to him with songs of praise! For the Lord is a great God, and a great King above all gods."
~ Psalm 95:2-3 (ESV)

"Enter his gates with thanksgiving; go into his courts with praise. Give thanks to him and praise his name."
~ Psalm 100:4 (NLT)

"Do not be anxious about anything, but in every situation, by prayer and petition, with thanksgiving, present your requests to God. And the peace of God, which transcends all understanding, will guard your hearts and your minds in Christ Jesus."
~ Philippians 4:6-7

What do these verses say about thanksgiving?
What else is involved?
Do you notice a pattern?

> Giving praise to God's name in song, joyful songs.
> Giving God more and more glory.
> Giving in every situation, by prayers and petitions, with thanksgiving.
> Giving thanks in all circumstances.

And finally, this verse inspires me to live with thanksgiving every moment of every day:

"Be thankful in all circumstances, for this is God's
will for you who belong to Christ Jesus."
~ 1 Thessalonians 5:18 (NLT)

This Bible verse shows how Jesus modeled the Cambridge Dictionary definition of thanksgiving:

"For I pass on to you what I received from the Lord himself. On the
night when he was betrayed, the Lord Jesus took some bread and gave
thanks to God for it. Then he broke it in pieces and said, 'This is my
body, which is given for you. Do this in remembrance of me.'"
~ 1 Corinthians 11:23-24 (NLT)

What a powerful Scripture. Jesus gave thanks to God even though He was going to suffer immense pain. He gave us the perfect example of thanksgiving, the "thanks" and "giving!" As Jesus celebrated the Last Supper with His disciples, He first gave thanks to God for the bread. Then He offered Himself, giving His body to you and me, commanding us to do this same thing in remembrance of Him.

It truly is an honor to celebrate the Eucharist, which in Greek means "thanksgiving." We express our thanks to Jesus for giving Himself and dying on the cross so we can spend eternity with Him.

What if, every day, we…

> thank God for who He is.
> thank God for all He has done and given.
> continually give thanks to God and give to others.

"Give thanks to the Lord, for he is good! His faithful love endures forever.
Cry out, 'Save us, O God of our salvation! Gather and rescue us from among
the nations, so we can thank your holy name and rejoice and praise you.'"
~ 1 Chronicles 16:34-35 (NLT)

54

One Way

We all face struggles, trials, and problems. They are a part of life. Have you noticed how some people handle difficulties or challenges better than others? Some people face difficulty through negativity, finding fault and complaining. Others have a positive outlook and see the bright side of life despite adversity.

There is one way to victoriously make it through the struggles, trials, and problems we face. That way is in truly knowing Jesus with our heart. This is the difference between night and day, darkness and light, famine, and feast.

When we truly know Christ with our heart, we can have a peace that surpasses all human understanding. This peace is rooted deep within our heart and rises to sustain us even in the most trying of circumstances.

Joy as big as an ocean can be ours each day. This joy comes from knowing Jesus is with us every step of the way and will never leave us. We don't let the immediate situation determine if we have joy. True joy is ours when God's promises become real to us.

To sum it up, no matter how many problems and struggles we have, we can live victoriously. Nobody can take away the peace and joy we can have by knowing Jesus as our Lord.

"Peace be with you, dear brothers and sisters, and may God the Father and the Lord Jesus Christ give you love with faithfulness. May God's grace be eternally upon all who love our Lord Jesus Christ."
~ Ephesians 6:23-24 (NLT)

55

Present Moment

God desires that we notice, embrace, and appreciate the gift of each moment, which puts joy in our heart that we can share with others. We have the power to brighten another's day with His love. Here are some ways I have acted on these thoughts.

My daughter and I stopped at a convenience store. While she ran in, I parked at the gas pump to wash my bug-splattered windshield. A man who coached my son several years earlier pulled up alongside my car. We hadn't talked in a few years. How nice it was to catch up on the news about our families.

I stopped at our car repair shop to deliver some "thank-you" cookies. I talked with an employee for about fifteen minutes, catching up on his hopes, dreams, and our families. I knew it was more important to be present in the moment than being concerned with my errands. It blessed my day.

My youngest son has a happy outlook on life and the gift of making people laugh and smile. He lives more in the present. He loves playing baseball but has had numerous injuries. At a follow-up doctor's appointment, while studying the skeletal and muscular posters on the wall, he had the idea to "play the doctor." Sitting on a stool near the door, he welcomed the orthopedic doctor into the room, introduced himself, and then slid the stool over to the desk. The doctor played along, with a big smile on his face, jumping right up on the examination table. My son explained the x-ray results, pretended to take notes, and told him what the patient needed to do to be able to play baseball again. The doctor could not stop smiling and gave my son a bear hug for playing the role so well. It was a priceless moment.

Be aware of the events God orchestrates in your life so you can glorify Him and share joy with others. And remember to notice and appreciate the present moment. Just embrace what is in front of you!

"Now listen! Today I am giving you a choice between life and death, between prosperity and disaster. For I command you this day to love the Lord your God and to keep his commands, decrees, and regulations by walking in his ways. If you do this, you will live and multiply, and the Lord your God will bless you and the land you are about to enter and occupy."
~ Deuteronomy 30:15-16 (NLT)

56

Love Not Shame

Jesus' death on the cross brought love into our lives, no longer shame! One definition of shame is: "A painful feeling of humiliation or distress caused by the consciousness of wrong or foolish behavior."

The earliest instance of shame is in the book of Genesis when Adam and Eve ate the fruit of the tree God told them not to eat.

> *"When the woman saw that the tree was good for*
> *food, and that it was a delight to the eyes,*
> *and that the tree was desirable to make one wise,*
> *she took some of its fruit and ate;*
> *and she also gave some to her husband with her, and he ate.*
> *Then the eyes of both of them were opened, and they*
> *knew that they were naked; and they sewed fig leaves*
> *together and made themselves waist coverings.*
> *Now they heard the sound of the Lord God walking in the garden in the*
> *cool of the day, and the man and his wife hid themselves from the presence*
> *of the Lord God among the trees of the garden. Then the Lord God called to*
> *the man, and said to him, 'Where are you?' He said, 'I heard the sound of*
> *You in the garden, and I was afraid because I was naked; so I hid myself.'"*
> ~ Genesis 3:6-10 (NASB)

Adam and Eve both experienced shame after eating the forbidden fruit. They were distressed at being naked and hid from the Lord because they knew they had done wrong. Never again would they have the unaltered oneness with God.

Christine M. Fisher

In the New Testament when Jesus was conceived through the power of the Holy Spirit, Joseph struggled with how to deal with shame.

> *"Now the birth of Jesus Christ was as follows: when His mother Mary had been betrothed to Joseph, before they came together she was found to be with child by the Holy Spirit. And Joseph her husband, being a righteous man and not wanting to disgrace her, planned to send her away secretly. But when he had considered this, behold, an angel of the Lord appeared to him in a dream, saying, 'Joseph, son of David, do not be afraid to take Mary as your wife; for the Child who has been conceived in her is of the Holy Spirit. She will bear a Son; and you shall call His name Jesus, for He will save His people from their sins.'"*
> ~ Matthew 1:18-21 (NASB)

Joseph, being a righteous man, did not want to expose Mary to shame, though he knew he did nothing wrong. After a dream, Joseph knew Mary was carrying the Savior of the world in her womb. It was all part of God's divine plan.

Jesus, the very one who came to show us such great love, was put to death, dying on the cross. He suffered one of the most shameful deaths precisely to show us the greatest love.

> *"Pilate then took Jesus and scourged Him. And the soldiers twisted together a crown of thorns and put it on His head, and put a purple robe on Him; and they began to come up to Him and say, 'Hail, King of the Jews!' and to give Him slaps in the face."*
> ~ John 19:1-3 (NASB)

Jesus was publicly disgraced, beaten and spit upon, nailed to a cross, and left to die a slow, painful death. Death by crucifixion was a humiliating experience reserved for the lowest of criminals. The Savior of the world, the one who saved us from our sins, left all shame at the cross for you and me. Jesus came to bring love and to take away our shame. Rejoice in that, my friends.

One definition of love is: "An intense feeling of deep affection."

Jesus is the epitome of love!

"But Jesus went to the Mount of Olives. At dawn he appeared again in the temple courts, where all the people gathered around him, and he sat down to teach them. The teachers of the law and the Pharisees brought in a woman caught in adultery. They made her stand before the group and said to Jesus, 'Teacher, this woman was caught in the act of adultery. In the Law Moses commanded us to stone such women. Now what do you say?' They were using this question as a trap, in order to have a basis for accusing him.

"But Jesus bent down and started to write on the ground with his finger. When they kept on questioning him, he straightened up and said to them, 'Let any one of you who is without sin be the first to throw a stone at her.' Again he stooped down and wrote on the ground. At this, those who heard began to go away one at a time, the older ones first, until only Jesus was left, with the woman still standing there. Jesus straightened up and asked her, 'Woman, where are they? Has no one condemned you?' 'No one, sir,' she said. 'Then neither do I condemn you,' Jesus declared. 'Go now and leave your life of sin.'"
~ John 8:1-11

Did that adulteress woman feel shamed by Jesus?
> No, not at all. She felt love from Jesus that changed her life from that day forward!

"The woman said to him, 'Sir, give me this water so that I won't get thirsty and have to keep coming here to draw water.' He told her, 'Go, call your husband and come back.' 'I have no husband,' she replied. Jesus said to her, 'You are right when you say you have no husband. The fact is, you have

Christine M. Fisher

had five husbands, and the man you now have is not your husband. What
you have just said is quite true.' 'Sir,' the woman said, 'I can see that you
are a prophet. Our ancestors worshiped on this mountain, but you Jews
claim that the place where we must worship is in Jerusalem.' 'Woman,' Jesus
replied, 'believe me, a time is coming when you will worship the Father
neither on this mountain nor in Jerusalem. You Samaritans worship what
you do not know; we worship what we do know, for salvation is from the
Jews. Yet a time is coming and has now come when the true worshipers
will worship the Father in the Spirit and in truth, for they are the kind
of worshipers the Father seeks. God is spirit, and his worshipers must
worship in the Spirit and in truth.' The woman said, 'I know that Messiah'
(called Christ) 'is coming. When he comes, he will explain everything
to us.' Then Jesus declared, 'I, the one speaking to you—I am he.'"
~ John 4:15-26

Despite the lifestyle of this Samaritan woman, did she feel shamed by
Jesus?

> No, not at all. He showed her love, which helped increase her faith
> to the point that she told everybody about Jesus.

"While Jesus was in one of the towns, a man came along who was covered
with leprosy. When he saw Jesus, he fell with his face to the ground and
begged him, 'Lord, if you are willing, you can make me clean.' Jesus
reached out his hand and touched the man. 'I am willing,' he said. 'Be
clean!' And immediately the leprosy left him. Then Jesus ordered him,
'Don't tell anyone, but go, show yourself to the priest and offer the sacrifices
that Moses commanded for your cleansing, as a testimony to them.'"
~ Luke 5:12-14

Did this leper feel shamed by Jesus?

> No, not at all. Rather, Jesus healed the man immediately, showing
> how much He loved the leper.

Can you think of instances when you have felt shame?

Was it shame personally inflicted or due to society's influence?

If personally inflicted due to sin, did you recognize your need for repentance and make things right?

Was it difficult to let go of the shame, despite Jesus' forgiveness, which is ours when we repent?

We read many Bible stories where society led people to think the person, or even the parents, must have committed a terrible sin that caused the issues. We know that is not the case, yet even to this day, society can inflict unjustified shame on us.

Through the first man and woman, Adam and Eve, shame was born. Through Jesus and His mother, Mary, love was born and came to reign. Jesus came to bring us love, healing, hope, peace, grace, and forgiveness – the ultimate solution to shame.

> *"But God demonstrates his own love for us in this:*
> *While we were still sinners, Christ died for us."*
> ~ Romans 5:8

57

Today

I receive daily emails from a coworker who gives me work to process. These emails end with a few encouraging words, something like, "Keep safe, enjoy the afternoon, or keep smiling." The closing on a recent email was, "Please be safe and enjoy today. It's another gift from God."

The thought spoke volumes to me, a great reminder of how we should be living each day.

How often do we go through life thinking about the future? What next big adventure do we have planned?

Scripture has messages for us in this regard:

"Do not boast about tomorrow, for you do not know what a day may bring."
~ Proverbs 27:1

"Now listen, you who say, 'Today or tomorrow we will go to this or that city, spend a year there, carry on business and make money.' Why, you do not even know what will happen tomorrow. What is your life? You are a mist that appears for a little while and then vanishes."
~ James 4:13-14

"So don't worry about tomorrow, for tomorrow will bring its own worries. Today's trouble is enough for today."
~ Matthew 6:34 (NLT)

The main messages are…

    tomorrow is not promised.
    we do not know what will happen day-to-day.
    focus on today.
    focus on tomorrow when it comes.

How important to live one day at a time, realizing it is a gift from God. If we always think and live in the future, we miss the blessing of today, the gift right in front of us.

How can we live in the present and realize what a gift today is?

> *"Be very careful, then, how you live—not as unwise but as wise, making the most of every opportunity, because the days are evil. Therefore do not be foolish, but understand what the Lord's will is."*
> ~ Ephesians 5:15-17

> *"Be wise in the way you act toward outsiders; make the most of every opportunity. Let your conversation be always full of grace, seasoned with salt, so that you may know how to answer everyone."*
> ~ Colossians 4:5-6

> *"But encourage one another daily, as long as it is called 'Today,' so that none of you may be hardened by sin's deceitfulness."*
> ~ Hebrews 3:13

We should…

    live wisely following God's will.
    see God working in every circumstance.
    let our words be grace-filled, thinking before we speak.
    encourage others in their faith journey.

When we receive a gift, we thank the giver and use the gift, which reminds us of the giver. Our daily lives should reflect these same principles as we thank God for the great gift of today. I recently heard someone say, "Life goes so fast. So often, we are in a rush to get to the next moment. We do not cherish the present moment, the gift of today. This day, this moment will never come back. Make happy moments today."

May these thoughts be a reminder for you to "enjoy today. It's another gift from God."

> *"And we know that in all things God works for the good of those who love him, who have been called according to his purpose."*
> ~ Romans 8:28

58

Perspective

The way we live is dependent on our perspective, outlook, and experiences. The Cambridge Dictionary defines perspective as: "A particular way of viewing things, which depends on one's experience and personality; the ability to consider things in relation to one another accurately and fairly. If something is in perspective, it is considered as part of a complete situation so that you have an accurate and fair understanding of it."

I believe our perspective of life is based on two main things:

How we view God…

What is your perspective of God?
How do you view Him?
Is God a distant, unapproachable judge who always condemns?

If we view Him in this way, our perspective might be that we cannot measure up to His expectations. We will always strive but never make the mark. It might seem that we need to "do" things, or act in a certain way, to earn God's love and maybe even our salvation.

Is God a close, loving, forgiving Father you know intimately?

If we view Him as one who loves and accepts us unconditionally, just as we are, this frees us. We do not need to earn His love or our salvation. Our relationship is one of mutual love, and we naturally want to share that with everyone we encounter. This kind of love leads to peace and joy, which is impossible to contain.

How we view life...

What is your perspective on life?
Is your life one of drudgery, where nothing seems to go right?
Is your world without hope and with negative thoughts?
Do you just exist day after day, going through the motions but not finding joy?

Or...

Do you find meaning in your identity as a child of God?
Do you know your purpose is to glorify Him in all you do?

If you view life as a child of God and an opportunity to glorify Him, you seek ways to share Christ and His love with those you meet. Even though there are many struggles, you know everything is okay because God is with you.

We make decisions based on our perspective, which means we can change our view of a situation if we make a conscious effort to change our perspective. When I have a positive perspective, I can see the Lord at work, even in the small things. A positive perspective helps me be open to others, taking time to love more and enjoy each moment.

Is the Lord showing you specific areas where you can change your perspective? Our challenge is to be in alignment with God's perspective, which is always "in perspective" because He sees the big picture. Keep seeking Him through the Word, fellowshipping with other Christians, and being open to the Spirit.

> "I am thankful for small mercies. I compared notes with one of my friends who expects everything of the universe and is disappointed when anything is less than the best, and I found that I begin at the other extreme, expecting nothing and am always full of thanks for moderate goods." –Ralph Waldo Emerson

God wants you to know: The world is as good as you see it is.

If your perspective is on the negative, you will see the bad.
> If your perspective is on the good, you will see goodness.
> Choose your perspective carefully.

> *"I will go home to my father and say, 'Father, I have sinned against both heaven and you, and I am no longer worthy of being called your son. Please take me on as a hired servant.' So he returned home to his father. And while he was still a long way off, his father saw him coming. Filled with love and compassion, he ran to his son, embraced him, and kissed him."*
> ~ Luke 15:18-20 (NLT)

59

Detours

I have experienced detours on my commute to work, which are inconvenient, usually involving extra time and travel.

Before a baseball tournament at a school campus, I went for a walk. Busy observing the beauty of the landscape, the huge buildings, and athletic complexes, I couldn't remember the turns I had taken. Nothing looked familiar and I didn't know which path lead back to the ball field. Words from a song echoed in my mind, "Ya gotta have a little faith." I needed faith to find my way back before the end of the game.

I finally came across two people who pointed me in the right direction. They were my angels in disguise, or so I thought. I followed their instructions and continued walking for a long time. Unfortunately, their directions had me turning left when I should have made a right, which added 40 minutes to my walk. Because of the detour, I missed part of the ball game.

What are some of the detours you have experienced in your walk with the Lord?

Maybe…

> it was a calling from the Lord that didn't come to fruition until later in life?
> you ignored the Lord calling you to live for Him instead of living for worldly desires?
> you started down a college or career path before realizing the Lord was leading a different direction?

What are some things we can learn from these detours?

> Detours are okay.
>
> Keep pressing on and seeking the way.
>
> Be patient and don't panic.
>
> Enjoy the scenery and the ride.
>
> Detours can produce great blessings.
>
> Keep the destination as the goal. It is not so important how we get there, but that we get there.

Things do not always go the way we think they should. Remember, it is God, not us, who is in control. When we get to our final destination, we will arrive with true happiness, contentment, success, and the knowledge in our heart of what our calling is and where we are supposed to be.

> *"Can anything ever separate us from Christ's love? Does it mean he no longer loves us if we have trouble or calamity, or are persecuted, or hungry, or destitute, or in danger, or threatened with death? (As the Scriptures say, 'For your sake we are killed every day; we are being slaughtered like sheep.') No, despite all these things, overwhelming victory is ours through Christ, who loved us."*
>
> ~ Romans 8:35-37 (NLT)

60

School

Did you know you are in school your entire life? Consider the following. The adventure of life is school. When we are born, our schooling begins. And guess what? It continues throughout life as we continue to learn, study, and center our lives in God. School is in session! Viewing life in this fashion can inspire our journey.

Our classroom is the beautiful world God created with its glorious sunrises and sunsets, colorful skies, majestic mountains, wildflowers, and animals. Everywhere we look, we see God's masterpieces and His presence.

Our earthly bodies are our schoolhouse. We never have to worry about going to a new building, learning our way around, or getting lost in our school.

Jesus is our teacher. How great it is that we have the same never-changing teacher throughout life's school experience. He is the ultimate, best teacher ever. And even better, He knows us oh, so well.

We are the students in this school of life. The way we live reflects what we learn. We have the privilege of learning new things every day, delving into a closer relationship with our Creator. All these things help us grow into the person God intends us to be.

There are many lessons we can learn, but we are to grow most in unconditional love, unconditional generosity, and unconditional forgiveness.

Do we love everyone unconditionally, no matter what they look like, what they do or how they treat us?

Do we give generously to those on the street who are homeless or the person who needs our time?

Do we forgive those who mistreat us?

We have opportunities to practice these lessons daily.

Our homework is in working through the problems of life, like suffering, trials, fear, anger, guilt, and pain. Our daily lessons and homework keep us learning, growing, and working through our problems. As we work through each day, we can study and learn God's way of thinking and living. We can read and study more of God's Word. We can be in communion with Him through prayer, devotionals, and encouraging posts to navigate through the issues and trials we face.

We need to be doing God's will no matter what we might think, want, or feel. We can release our fears, anger, guilt, and pain. When problems occur, we need to use our knowledge as to the best way to work through them. And remember, our homework isn't always perfect.

Tests and quizzes happen, sometimes even pop quizzes, when we least expect them, to help us see if we are on the right track. These tests and pop quizzes give us opportunities to trust God's sovereignty.

When problems occur, whether large or small, do we remember what we have been studying?

Do we put into practice the things we have learned through our homework assignments?

Do we trust the Lord?

Do we let fear and anxiety overtake us?

Or do we have faith in God who is bigger than our problems? God can even calm the sea.

Every day there is some time for recess, those times we are at peace with God and the world. Those times we might go for a quick walk or bike ride to refocus, observe God's creation, or connect with Him, our life source. In these times, be like a young child running, letting go, and being free.

Summer vacations offer longer times of peace, joy and love to "just be." We can enjoy the quietness with no routine or schedule. We take time to relax, renew, and be still. What a great benefit to trust in the Lord. It is a taste of what heaven will be like. Take time to enjoy the scenery, knowing you are God's creation too.

We earn our diploma when we are ready for graduation. We are continually learning to trust God completely, no matter what we think or feel. We choose to let go of control. We need to keep working on it until we die.

At graduation, we leave our schoolhouse. We celebrate our commencement, leaving this earth and going to our eternal home. We have the privilege of living with God for eternity, celebrating who we are in Him, forever in His arms.

It was a God moment when I was skimming a Young Life newsletter. There was an article talking about one of the Presidents of Young Life who recently lost his life. It said, "To use a favorite phrase of his, '(he) was graduated to glory.'"

Be encouraged to put into practice unconditional love, unconditional generosity, and unconditional forgiveness. This is what Jesus modeled for us. Keep doing your homework so you are always prepared when quizzes or tests come your way. And always be prepared to graduate to glory.

"By this all people will know that you are my
disciples, if you have love for one another."
~ John 13:35 (ESV)

61

Through His Power

One of the hardest things is to remain calm and peaceful when going through the trials of life. The world needs to see Christians trusting God, possessing, and expressing joy and peace, even during the rough, rocky times. We do this through His power.

"May the God of hope fill you with all joy and peace as you trust in him, so that you may overflow with hope by the power of the Holy Spirit."
~ Romans 15:13

As Christians, we need to repeatedly surrender our lives to God, which is difficult because it requires us to put complete trust in our Savior. He is our Creator and is quite capable of leading us, being in control of each circumstance.

"Then Jesus said to his disciples, 'Whoever wants to be my disciple must deny themselves and take up their cross and follow me. For whoever wants to save their life will lose it, but whoever loses their life for me will find it.'"
~ Matthew 16:24-25

We all endure trials and suffer in different ways. Even Jesus willingly experienced many trials, temptations, and sufferings. It was all part of God's plan for our salvation.

"Consider it pure joy, my brothers and sisters, whenever you face trials of many kinds, because you know that the testing of your faith produces perseverance."
~ James 1:2-3

During our times of trial and suffering, we need to depend on God and His strength to make it through. He is not a God who rejoices in our suffering. He waits for us to grab onto Him and draw from His power. Difficult situations make us realize our need for Him.

"God is our refuge and strength, an ever-present help in trouble."
~ Psalm 46:1

"I have told you these things, so that in me you may have peace. In this world you will have trouble. But take heart! I have overcome the world."
~ John 16:33

When we reach out to God, not relying on ourselves, we are different from the rest of the world. We can experience joy and peace through the trials of life. May you thank God for the hard times and the peace you experience when you know His presence and love are leading you.

"Dear brothers and sisters, I close my letter with these last words: Be joyful. Grow to maturity. Encourage each other. Live in harmony and peace. Then the God of love and peace will be with you."
~ 2 Corinthians 13:11 (NLT)

62

Longing

Can you remember times in life when you longed for something?

Was it...

> for a baby you wanted to make your family complete?
> for a child to return home after a semester at college?
> waiting to hear from a loved one in the path of a natural disaster?
> to save up enough money to buy the house you wanted?
> to get a long-awaited letter in the mail from a loved one far away?
> hoping to be acknowledged by someone famous?
> counting down the days until a loved one returned from deployment
> and you were able to hold them in your arms again?

Do you remember the feelings or emotions you felt as the longing came closer to fruition?

Did...

> the longing become stronger as each day passed?
> you want it so badly, that if wishing could make it happen, it
> would have happened right then?
> each day seem like an eternity?
> you start to wonder if the longing would come true?
> it release a new passion in you to be more sensitive to others going
> through trials?
> it make you more patient through your waiting?

In thinking about the longings and emotions, consider how much the Lord truly longs for you every day to...

> know Him intimately.
> love Him with all your heart.
> serve Him in all you do.
> acknowledge Him at work in you, in your life, and in others.
> see Him in all Creation.
> talk with Him.
> praise Him in all things.
> embrace the unconditional, everlasting love He offers.
> put Him first in your life.
> see Him working all things together for your good, according to His plan.

Your loving Father, God, truly longs for you. His love for you is so great. He longs for you to commune continually with Him. He longs for you even more than the greatest longing you have ever experienced.

> *"In all their suffering he also suffered, and he personally*
> *rescued them. In his love and mercy he redeemed them. He*
> *lifted them up and carried them through all the years."*
> ~ Isaiah 63:9 (NLT)

63

The Labyrinth of Life

I received these thoughts and insights from a retreat at one of my favorite holy places. The theme of the weekend was "Our Spiritual Journey," and the visual was a labyrinth, which represents wholeness. A labyrinth has only one path that leads to the center, and there is only one way in and out. It does not have any dead ends and has a single route, despite the many twists and turns.

What if we looked at a labyrinth as life on earth? The center of the labyrinth represents God. The one way into the labyrinth could symbolize your birth. When you are born, you begin your entrance into the labyrinth of life.

How appropriate
that labyrinths represent
wholeness;

a wholeness that we have with
God at the center of our lives;

seeking His purpose for our life
on this earth;

walking minute by minute
with Him.

Christine M. Fisher

You reach the center of the labyrinth when you come to the point of knowing Jesus as your personal Lord and Savior. It is knowing Jesus in your heart, not just "head" knowledge about Him. With Him, you become filled with God's Spirit, grace, mercy, and love.

As you navigate the many twists and turns through the different stages of life, your focus and eyes should always be on the center, God.

No matter where you go, what direction, what path you take, you can always see God working in each stage of your life.

As long as you keep your eyes on God, you will be fine. Once you reach the center of the labyrinth, you get to journey back and forth.

What might you realize in doing this?

You are walking with God in this labyrinth of life. God is always with you leading and guiding. Look for Him. Each day can be considered a day in the labyrinth of life. May it remind you God is always walking with you. Keep your eyes on God, the center. In the labyrinth of life, you can't get lost if you keep your eyes on the center.

Those who walk with God always reach their destination.

Consider spending a few moments contemplating your spiritual journey. Think about the many twists and turns you've experienced. See how God has blessed you and has been with you leading you every step of the way. You are loved.

"Always remember this: life is a journey. It is a path, a journey to meet Jesus." –Pope Francis

Journey back out, spreading God's love and goodness to others.

"And now, Israel, what does the Lord your God ask
of you but to fear the Lord your God,
to walk in obedience to him, to love him, to serve the Lord your God
with all your heart and with all your soul."
~ Deuteronomy 10:12

Christine M. Fisher

64

The Glove

Do you have a glove handy? Get it, please.

Do you have a free hand? Sure, put that phone down, just for a few seconds.

Now carefully slip the glove over your hand.

Take a few minutes and look at the glove on your hand.

Consider the glove is God your loving Father. Consider your life is the hand.

May this glove's visual be a reminder to you that…

the Lord is always with you.
He will never leave you orphaned.
the Lord will never forsake you.
you are one with the Lord.
you are made in God's image.
the Lord will always direct your path.
He is constantly molding and shaping you.
at times, the Lord will stretch you out of your comfort zone.
God is always protecting you.
nothing is going to happen to you that God can't handle.

When you see a glove, may you be reminded of G(od's) LOVE for you. When you feel discouraged, remember the glove and let it remind you how precious you are to God.

"Because he holds fast to me in love, I will deliver him;
I will protect him, because he knows my name.
When he calls to me, I will answer him;
I will be with him in trouble; I will rescue him and honor him."
~ Psalm 91:14-15 (ESV)

65

Opportunity Clock

I heard the phrase "opportunity clock" while conversing with a gal from my high school years. I was in awe God brought us together after more than a quarter of a century.

In school, we exchanged a casual "hello" now and then, but we never talked much. We connected through Facebook a few years ago. I was intrigued to learn she was inspired to write the music and script for a musical called "Ascend," which explores the resurrection of Jesus. We connected when she had staged readings, and it was an honor to attend the first performance of the musical.

We bumped into each other at another event and decided to have lunch together. As she said, "We share a love for our Lord that unites us."

During our conversation, she shared this thought:

> For those who set our clocks to wake us up in the morning, why do we call it an alarm clock?
> Do we really want to view it as an alarm? An alarm usually signifies something bad is happening, like when a fire alarm sounds.
> Do we want to start our day with a lingering alarm thought? Isn't it more pleasant to think of it as setting our opportunity clock to awaken for fresh opportunities?

Opportunities to…

> shine the light of Christ through the darkness.
> share Christ in us with other people.

converse with our Lord and Savior.
see God at work in everything and everyone.
praise our Creator for His goodness.
love our neighbor.

When you awaken in the morning, what is the first thing that goes through your mind?

Is it a list of the things to do?
How will you get everywhere on time?
Or do you awaken and say, "Lord, what opportunities await me today? In what ways will you reveal yourself to me? How can I reveal you to others?"

I encourage you to look for the opportunities the Lord puts in your path each day.

"And you must love the Lord your God with all your heart, all your soul, all your mind, and all your strength. The second is equally important: Love your neighbor as yourself. No other commandment is greater than these."
~ Mark 12:30-31 (NLT)

Christine M. Fisher

66

Reckless Abandon

Our family planned an excursion vacation in Aruba. Driving a UTV (utility terrain vehicle) is outside my comfort zone, so we planned on having our daughter do the driving. Unfortunately, we were informed she did not meet the age requirement, so I became the second driver. Needless to say, I doubted myself and my ability.

Before taking off, we had to sign a waiver form, which mentioned the vehicle could easily topple over, so using caution was important. We had a one-minute crash course on how to drive the one-gear, which is high gear, UTV. I asked our guide, Rocky, for reassurance that anyone could handle the vehicle. His answer, "If you can drive, you can do it, but you do have to be forceful and bold."

The UTV's were open-air vehicles without mirrors, windshields, or directional signals. When turning left, the driver uses the proper hand signal, and when turning right, the passenger does. There was no way to move the seat forward, so I had to adjust myself, sitting on the edge of the seat, so I could reach the pedals. I opted to wear a helmet just in case I toppled our UTV but didn't have enough time to adjust the strap before starting our convoy of eight.

We didn't know the excursion was called "Shake & Roll" until we reached the lot where the UTVs were parked. We also didn't know red dust, sand, and dirt would accompany our adventure until we were given bandannas to protect our nose and mouth. And we certainly didn't know we would be driving on the paved roads of Aruba, along with the regular traffic before reaching the off-road portion.

The three-hour adventure began. Since I was apprehensive about driving the UTV, I drove directly behind Rocky, focusing my attention on him. I'm sure it was hilarious watching my UTV putt-putt-puttering along until I got the hang of pushing the pedal as far as it would go. It reminded me of driving antique cars at an amusement park. We were on the paved roads for fifteen minutes. I was relieved to see the Arubans drive on the same side of the road as we do.

Suddenly we turned onto an unpaved road, an almost sandy area, where the real adventure started. It was amazing and breathtaking to see cacti and desert, and rocky areas around the northern part of Aruba. Shortly after our first stop, we flipped on the 4-wheel drive knob, and off we went.

I kept thinking, "Okay, just keep following Rocky. If he goes fast, you go fast, and if he slows down, you slow down." Eventually, the thought of "reckless abandon" ran through my head. I had to keep going forward with reckless abandon; there was no other choice. Whatever was going to happen would happen.

By our next stop, Rocky gave me a thumbs up and said I was doing great. I think he was surprised I was keeping up through the rough, rocky, sandy terrain. The view was incredible. We saw mountains, a fort, a lighthouse, the ocean where locals go because of the intense waves, and a church. What a beautiful earth God made for us to enjoy.

What are some lessons I learned from this UTV experience that relate to our walk with the Lord?

We need to follow God with reckless abandon. Reckless means "having or showing no regard for danger or consequences." Abandon means "showing lack of restraint." This means we surrender to Him with all our being, with no regard for anything else. It means we allow Him to lead and guide us in everything, and we cling to and trust Him as the author of life.

How do we do this?

By…

> stepping out of our comfort zone.
> being strong and courageous.
> only looking forward–not backward or to the side (no mirrors!)
> following only the Lord, not getting sidetracked.
> enjoying the beauty all around us.
> giving the Lord all we have.
> pursuing Him with reckless abandon.

What does it look like to pursue the Lord with reckless abandon?

> Focusing our thoughts and actions on Him, not ourselves.
> Keeping our eyes on Him and His ways, not the ways of this world.
> Letting God define us, not our present circumstances.
> Embracing the eternal, not our temporary, dreams for this life.
> Loving everyone passionately as God loves us, because He made us all.

Is the Lord calling you to work on any of the areas listed above? Be encouraged to step out in faith and take baby steps to accomplish it.

> Follow the Lord with reckless abandon!

"For this reason I remind you to fan into flame the gift of God, which is in you through the laying on of my hands, for God gave us a spirit not of fear but of power and love and self-control."
~ 2 Timothy 1:6-7 (ESV)

67

You've Got a Friend

Are you familiar with the song, *You've Got a Friend* ³ by Carole King? The lyrics remind me of our relationship with the Lord. Here are the words to the chorus:

> You just call out my name
> And you know wherever I am
> I'll come running to see you again.

What a perfect description of Jesus, the only true, dependable friend. Think about it.

Who is always there…

> when you're down and troubled?
> when you need some love and care?
> to brighten your darkest night?
> when the storm clouds come?
> knocking on your door?
> when others turn cold, hurtful, and desert you?

Yes, Jesus! All we need to do, at any time, is to call His name. And He will come running. He is there for us, our one, true, unfailing friend. The song also speaks to me, inspiring me to try to be that friend to others. In our humanness, we will at times fail others, but striving to be a friend like Jesus is a good thing.

"A friend loves at all times, and a brother is born for a time of adversity."
~ Proverbs 17:17

Christine M. Fisher

Section 4

GOD'S LOVE
ILLUMINATED IN
MINISTRY

"Dear children, let's not merely say that we love each other;
let us show the truth by our actions."
~ 1 John 3:18 (NLT)

The way we love God carries over into the way we live our daily lives. We serve the Lord with our words, the way we love, and the things we do.

Our actions can take the form of official ministries within churches and organizations. Ministry can be praying for others, picking up trash you see while walking, and caring for the earth with respect. Ministry is a way of life. Our actions need to show we belong to God and experience His love. All we do should reflect the glory of God.

God's love illuminated in ministry.

68

A Gift to Give

A smile will do so much
to brighten someone's day.
And a hug will make such
a warm difference in today.

You might send a card
that says just what you feel.
And the receiver won't find it hard
to make the feeling lasting and real.

If you listen for a while,
you'll show someone you care.
When you see that smile,
you'll know the problem is easier to bear.

So let's begin today
and reach out in God's love
to brighten someone else's day
with graces from above.

"Dear friends, let us love one another, for love comes from God.
Everyone who loves has been born of God and knows God."
~ 1 John 4:7

69

His Embrace

Through the years, I've earned the title of "Put the baby to sleep gal." Well, that is probably true for all babies, except my own. It was more difficult with them. I like to think I earned the title by my calming, peaceful influence on the babies, certainly not because I'm boring.

I enjoy holding a loving and innocent baby, singing softly to them, and snuggling them close, as they fall asleep. It is a great time to pray for them. Before I was a mother, I would snuggle my niece and she would fall asleep in my arms, so peaceful and content.

A touching moment was when my grandnephew was fighting the sleep, squirming around. As I held him, he snuggled in close on my shoulder and peacefully slept. It made me think how he had enough trust in me and was comfortable enough to drift to sleep.

Another time when I was trying to get him to sleep, I decided to get away from the crowd gathered outside. As I walked toward the sidewalk, I saw our reflection in a car window. It reminded me of how much God, our Father, waits for us to come to Him, to wrap His arms around us, and love us. He wants to embrace us as we rest in His loving, caring arms. God wants us to know everything is okay, and He is there to protect us. We need to put our trust in His mighty ways and be comfortable turning to Him.

Remember to reach out to God, our loving Father, especially during the challenging times. He is always there, waiting to embrace us with His loving arms wrapped tightly around us. Everything will be okay with Him protecting us. Trust in His ways.

"I love you, Lord; you are my strength.
The Lord is my rock, my fortress, and my savior; my God is my rock,
in whom I find protection. He is my shield, the power that saves me,
and my place of safety."
~ Psalm 18:1-2 (NLT)

70

Be the Angel

For the past three years, my youngest son, Caleb, has attended a Christian music festival camp. Each year he returns with "God moments" to share. At his most recent festival, he was introduced to a girl, and they hit it off, both enjoying roller coasters and having similar interests and personalities.

Caleb learned his new friend was living with a relative because of family dynamics. He shared, "She genuinely cares about everyone and how they feel. She doesn't have much money and her life has not been easy." He continued, "She's so generous to other campers. When asked why she is willing to be generous and spend what little she has to care for others, she replied, 'God will provide.'"

While at camp, Caleb texted me, "I was at the concert the first night of the festival, after meeting this new friend, and a thought popped into my mind. I want to pay her festival entry fee out of my own money." We both knew it was the Holy Spirit prompting him.

I suggested he talk to the leader-in-charge and work out a refund for his new friend and then pay the fee from his money. I wanted to make sure a refund could be worked out. He insisted, "I got this Mom. Trust me."

When I picked Caleb up from camp, I brought his money in an envelope. He wrote a note, inserted it into the envelope, and gave it to his friend as she was leaving. He said he was shaking when he wrote the note and did not remember what he had written. When I questioned him later about why he didn't want to go through the leader, he said, "The fewer people who know about this, the better." His answer gave me a new perspective.

Later that evening, she called my son in tears, thanking him for the gift and for his friendship. Then she said, "I wasn't going to attend the festival because it marks the second anniversary of my friend's suicide. I struggled with going to an amusement park on a day that held so much heartache. When I finally made the decision to go, I asked God to send an angel while I was at the festival to help me get through the difficult time. God answered my prayer by bringing you into my life. The things you said and did helped boost my spirit, faith, and belief in God and myself. I don't know what I'm going to do with this money – I think I'm either going to pay it forward or put it toward starting my own business one day." Caleb said this was a defining moment in his faith journey and his faith had grown stronger.

When Caleb came home from the camping trip he said, "Mom, this is a long, crazy story, and you're going to want to write about this!"

After he proofed the rough draft, he suggested I add some reflection questions:

> When is the last time you felt the Spirit leading you to do something?
> Did you follow through?
> When you have received a special blessing, have you, too, felt like paying it forward?
> When has someone been an angel in your life?
> How can you be an angel in someone's life?
> When was a time you were in need and knew that God would provide?
> When have you shared the joy of the Lord with a stranger?

"I led them with cords of human kindness, with ties of love. To them I was like one who lifts a little child to the cheek, and I bent down to feed them."
~ Hosea 11:4

71

Blinded

"Rest my child,
you have not need fear the dark.
My arms will hold you like the ark
and keep you from harm."
Lyrics from *Greater Than You Know*[4]

"My sheep listen to my voice; I know them and they
follow me. I give them eternal life and they will never
perish; no one can snatch them out of my hand."
~ John 10:27-28 (NLT)

The lyric above is from a song by independent musician, Weston Skaggs. The Bible verse was from a meaningful sermon, which brought tears to my eyes. I heard it at church before heading to my Neonatal Intensive Care Unit (NICU) ministry where I love and hold the babies who get off to a rough start.

After arriving at the NICU, I scrubbed up and held a little boy. He was bundled in a "blue light mat," which is sometimes necessary for newborns who exhibit signs of jaundice. The headband was a blindfold over his eyes to protect them from the bright lights, which reminded me to tell him, "You have no need to fear the dark." I whispered, "God is protecting you. This darkness will only be temporary."

Holding the somewhat bulky mat, sometimes I needed to wrap both arms around him, along with the different tubes connected to his little body. I again whispered, "My arms will hold you like the ark, to keep you from harm."

I reflected on how the Scripture verses I heard earlier that morning applied to this little guy. I hoped the sound of my voice was a soothing reassurance that everything was going to be okay. I am sure he knows his shepherd's voices (his parents). When they come to visit, I bet it soothes him even more, hearing their familiar voices, possibly even bringing a smile to his face. No one or nothing could snatch the comfort and safety of that little one.

Gazing upon his face, not knowing the color or shape of his eyes, made me wonder:

> How often are we blinded to God's love or presence in our life?
> How long do we reject God though He reveals Himself in even the simple, little things?
> Sometimes we are blinded for years before we come to know God and accept Him as our Lord.

Then I wondered:

> Are we blinded to people He puts in our path we could minister to or bless?
> Do we continually see Him guiding and directing each step of our life?

In case you need encouragement, remember:

> You do not need to fear the dark.
> His arms are holding you like the ark.
> He will keep you from harm.
> To listen to His voice foremost in your life.
> To keep following His lead.
> Eternal life is yours.
> You will never perish.
> You are safe in His hand; no one can snatch you out of His hand!

"But let all who take refuge in you rejoice; let them sing joyful praises forever. Spread your protection over them, that all who love your name may be filled with joy."
~ Psalm 5:11 (NLT)

72

An Unexpected Phone Call

At the soup kitchen where my family volunteers, there is a gentleman who serves with us and handles the drinks. He has many health and emotional problems. Through the years, I have gained a greater appreciation for him. He is thoughtful, and a good Christian example. His heart is in the right place, which is most important.

One evening he called to wish us a nice vacation. I was impressed he remembered we wouldn't be there that day and took the time to call and wish us a nice vacation. His one-minute phone call made me feel special. He also remembers us during the holidays when he calls to wish us a Merry Christmas or a Happy Thanksgiving.

His actions remind me: It doesn't take much time to make a difference in someone's life. The simplest things can be such a blessing. A simple one-minute phone call made my day.

Are there ways you can make a difference? It might be a simple phone call to let someone know you are praying for them. Perhaps it's dropping off cookies for your mechanic. Be creative and see what God leads you to do.

"Therefore if you have any encouragement from being united with Christ, if any comfort from his love, if any common sharing in the Spirit, if any tenderness and compassion, then make my joy complete by being like-minded, having the same love, being one in spirit and of one mind."
~ Philippians 2:1-2

Christine M. Fisher

73

Missionary Disciple

I recently saw something at church entitled "A Prayer for Missionary Discipleship." I have always considered a missionary disciple as one who goes to other countries to proclaim the gospel message to those who have not heard. This prayer has expanded my thoughts of what a Missionary Disciple is.

A missionary is a person sent by a church into an area to carry on evangelism or other activities, such as educational or hospital work. All Christians, as followers of Christ, are called to evangelize by the way we live. No matter what we are doing or who we interact with, we are evangelizing. It is the things we do, why we do them, and how we do them.

A disciple is any follower of Christ, which means we first love Him, with all our heart and mind, and live to point others toward Him. We naturally want others to have that relationship with Jesus, to love Him and worship Him with all their heart.

Simply stated, a missionary disciple is a follower of Christ, sent to carry on evangelism. Does that mean you, my friend, are a missionary disciple? I am a missionary disciple and I bet you are too!

Read the following prayer, which I think is a powerful way to live daily, as we are missionary disciples.

A Prayer for Missionary Discipleship

Lord Jesus, throughout Sacred Scripture
you encouraged your disciples to
"seek and you will find,"
"knock and it shall be opened to you."
Allow me, your follower,
to begin to be formed in Your Spirit by seeking answers through You,
being evangelized in Your truth,
being converted through Your mercy,
and being led to You to become Your Missionary Disciple,
the one You send out into our community so
that others might come to know You
and accept the kingdom of God.
I ask this through Christ our Lord. Amen.

*"Ask and it will be given to you; seek and you will find; knock and the
door will be opened to you. For everyone who asks receives; the one who
seeks finds; and to the one who knocks, the door will be opened."*
~ Matthew 7:7-8

We can be formed in His Spirit by earnestly and continually seeking Him
in prayer. We become evangelized in His truths by reading the Word,
applying it in our lives, and sharing with others. We are converted through
His mercy by receiving God's forgiveness through Jesus. We all encounter,
come to know, and accept the kingdom of God because of our life and
example.

Consider these two thoughts:

We are called to be missionaries to the extent we have encountered
the love of God in Christ Jesus.

We are challenged, every day, to be actively engaged in evangelization. If we have truly experienced God's saving love, our mission is to go out and proclaim His love to all we meet.

A friend summed it up this way:

Missionary discipleship = today making God known
however I can,
wherever I am,
to whoever is there,
with whatever I have,
and tomorrow do it again.

So, what are you waiting for? Go, be that missionary disciple every day of your life!

"Above all, love each other deeply, because love covers over a multitude of sins. Offer hospitality to one another without grumbling. Each of you should use whatever gift you have received to serve others, as faithful stewards of God's grace in its various forms."
~ 1 Peter 4:8-10

74

Encourage One Another

It is an honor and privilege to encourage others in their walk with the Lord. God has entrusted us, His children, with that responsibility. The simple ways we share Christ and offer encouragement to others are just as important as being a missionary in a foreign country.

A quick Google search of the word encouragement yields these definitions: "The action of giving someone support, confidence, or hope; persuasion to do or to continue something; the act of trying to stimulate the development of an activity, state, or belief."

"For God has not destined us for wrath, but to obtain salvation through our Lord Jesus Christ, who died for us so that whether we are awake or asleep we might live with him. Therefore encourage one another and build one another up, just as you are doing. We ask you, brothers, to respect those who labor among you and are over you in the Lord and admonish you, and to esteem them very highly in love because of their work. Be at peace among yourselves. And we urge you, brothers, admonish the idle, encourage the fainthearted, help the weak, be patient with them all."
~ 1 Thessalonians 5:9-14 (ESV)

"And let's consider how to encourage one another in love and good deeds, not abandoning our own meeting together, as is the habit of some people, but encouraging one another; and all the more as you see the day drawing near."
~ Hebrews 10:24-25 (NASB)

"Take care, brothers and sisters, that there will not be in any one of you an evil, unbelieving heart that falls away from the living God. But

Christine M. Fisher

encourage one another every day, as long as it is still called "today,"
so that none of you will be hardened by the deceitfulness of sin."
~ Hebrews 3:12-13 (NASB)

These Bible passages teach us that encouragement is vital.

We encourage others...

> to live for the Lord.
> who might be lacking in courage.
> to help them reach their potential.
> to worship together and grow in faith.
> to turn from evil and sin.
> to have faith, not doubt.

My faith walk has been encouraged through simple acts of kindness by people who might not realize the impact of their gesture.

One day I was sitting in church, praying. Someone came from behind, put their arms around my shoulders, and hugged me. The woman did not say a word. The Lord used her gesture to bless and minister to me about a situation that seemed hopeless.

Another time a friend spoke words of affirmation about a situation, saying, "Don't give up hope." My human perspective didn't think things would work out favorably. I held on to her words, and God did what I thought was impossible.

A woman and I exchanged hugs as we were leaving church one day. She whispered in my ear, "Thank you for sending me your writings. They always come at just the right time." I couldn't help but thank God for working, inspiring, and leading me to help spread His love and goodness.

It was an encouragement one day when a friend said, "One of the biggest compliments we can give is to tell someone they remind us of Christ. I just want to let you know, I see Christ in you."

Can you recall a time when you were encouraged by another's words or gestures? I have a challenge for you. Try to consciously encourage at least one person daily.

You might do this by:

Affirming a strength you see in their character.
Thanking someone whose spiritual gift or talent has blessed you.
Listening to and offering words of affirmation
to someone who is struggling.
Affirming those making positive changes to continue their journey.

Yes, encouraging another is something we can
all do! Ready, set, go! Encourage!

*"Your love has given me great joy and encouragement, because
you, brother, have refreshed the hearts of the Lord's people."*
~ Philemon 1:7

75

My Little Buddy

While holding babies in the NICU, I had a special encounter with my little buddy who I bonded with over several weeks. He was born full-term at a birth weight of 2 pounds and 7 ounces. I was happy to see his face look fuller as he gained weight, but it was difficult to see him fussy and unhappy. One day, as I tried to soothe him, holding him close, the nurse took his vitals and fed him. I learned he would be going home soon and could sense this was my last day holding him. It was a bittersweet moment.

Later that morning, I snuggled a baby girl for a while. Even though my little buddy was two nursery sections away, I could hear him crying. When I was free, I walked toward his bassinette and saw a nurse trying to comfort him. When I approached, she let me pick him up and hold him. It took a long time to calm him as I ran through my gamut of songs.

Then I began repeating his name. He became quiet, closing his eyes, resting peacefully in my arms. As I rocked him and remembered our two months together, a flood of tears came to my eyes. The emotions of loving this little guy, pondering his future and life, were all released. God's presence was there. To the amazement of the nurses, he was finally quiet, peacefully sleeping for the first time that day. What an honor God used me to calm him, bringing my little buddy a few moments of peace. He will always have a special place in my heart, and I continue to pray for him and his family.

This encounter made me think about the difficult seasons in our lives and how unfair, bad things will happen. It may be the loss of a friendship, the death of a loved one, or an incurable disease that presents. These things may make us feel like kicking and screaming, like my little buddy did when he was fussy and unhappy. It may even turn into a pleading with the Lord.

> How do you handle the difficult times?
> Who or what soothes you?
> Do you turn to coping mechanisms, like addictions?
> Do you complain to others or dwell on the negative?
> Maybe you turn to trusted friends who will be honest and encourage you with truth.

I have learned the best way is to cry out to Jesus, telling Him about the pain and asking for help. We can find peace despite trying circumstances. We can stand on the promises of God, our Father, spend more time in prayer, and recall His faithfulness throughout our life.

The next time you go through a hardship, be encouraged to let the presence of God fill you, seeking the peace only He can give. Reach out to the people who will support you, soothe you, and encourage you. Most of all, I pray you may hear the Lord gently calling your name, assuring you that you are resting safely in His arms.

> *"But now, O Jacob, listen to the Lord who created you. O Israel, the one who formed you says, 'Do not be afraid, for I have ransomed you. I have called you by name; you are mine. When you go through deep waters, I will be with you. When you go through rivers of difficulty, you will not drown. When you walk through the fire of oppression, you will not be burned up; the flames will not consume you. Others were given in exchange for you. I traded their lives for yours because you are precious to me. You are honored, and I love you.'"*
> ~ Isaiah 43:1-2, 4 (NLT)

Christine M. Fisher

76

Share the Pain

Each day we meet people who are hurting, struggling to find their way. We all experience pain or heartache at different times in life. The pain can run the gamut from physical to emotional to mental. We might not "see" the pain with our eyes, but listening to people with our ears and heart, might help us understand what they are experiencing.

How about you?

Do you find that it helps to share your pain with another?

Sometimes it's too much to bear alone.

Human interaction helps because a trusted friend can show compassion and understanding for what you are going through.

Are you aware when others are struggling?

Do you take the time to understand what they are going through?

Or do you step away, thinking you cannot help them?

Lending an ear or sharing some of your life experiences could be just the thing someone needs to help them bear the pain. By caring about someone else's pain, you might be the difference between life and death for them. Try to be more aware of the needs of others and do what you can to help them walk out their journey.

"When God puts love and compassion on your heart toward someone, He's offering you an opportunity to make a difference in that person's life. You must learn to follow that love. Don't ignore it. Act on it. Somebody needs what you have." –Spiritual Inspiration

> *"Finally, all of you should be of one mind. Sympathize with each other. Love each other as brothers and sisters. Be tenderhearted, and keep a humble attitude."*
> ~ 1 Peter 3:8 (NLT)

77

Saying Yes

The book of Jonah is only four chapters long. A brief synopsis of the book of Jonah follows:

> Jonah was a prophet, someone who shares specific, divinely inspired messages from the Lord. God asked Jonah to go to Nineveh and share His message with the people. Jonah did not want the city of Nineveh to repent and be saved so, rather than obeying God, he fled and boarded a ship headed to a faraway city. A great storm arose on the sea, and Jonah confessed he was running from God. The shipmates cast Jonah overboard, and he was swallowed by a whale. As he sat in the belly of the whale, Jonah called out to God and repented of his disobedience. The whale, after three days and three nights, spit Jonah out on dry land. Jonah submitted to God and went to Nineveh, sharing His message of warning and repentance. Jonah, reluctant yet obedient to God, spoke God's words and the entire city of Nineveh, with more than 120,000 inhabitants, repented. And just as Jonah suspected, God had mercy on the city and did not destroy it.

From this story, we see the importance of obedience to God. We also see the importance of following God's lead in our lives and ministries. If we, like Jonah, don't initially obey, God is always ready with His loving, open arms, to accept us when we repent.

> How often does God call us to step out in faith to further His kingdom?

How often are we obedient to those little promptings the Holy Spirit gives?

How willing are we to challenge ourselves, stepping outside our comfort zone, to say yes to a new adventure in our faith journey?

Writing and publishing weekly thoughts is one of my ministries, where I am able to share my faith, evangelize, and help others see God in the ordinary. He has led and opened doors for me to publish online weekly inspirations since September 2014. These posts have evolved into the birth of two books, which was never on my bucket list, but God put people in my path to make it come to fruition.

Publishing my first book, *God's Presence Illuminated,* led to a new adventure, a book launch. My Pastor showed enthusiasm and moral support from the moment I first mentioned the book. Public speaking is not one of my gifts, but I mustered the courage to say yes to God in talking about my book in front of an audience.

I felt God leading and challenging me to grow by sharing in front of a crowd. I spoke about my faith journey and the many ways God has shown Himself through the process of writing my book. Despite the pandemic, twenty people came to the launch to show their support. It was a time of joyful obedience to God, where I felt loved and valued by Him and others.

After the book launch, my mind went to the negative of how it could have been better. "My voice was too shaky. I talked too fast. Toward the end, my voice was too quiet." Then I was able to turn those thoughts to the positive. "I did my best. I was obedient and gave it my all." One friend summed it up well, sharing, "Honestly, I know speaking is not your forté, but you did it with grace! Your emotion came through." I was grateful for that affirmation and the encouragement from others. Often, we are too hard on ourselves.

Writing a book and publicly launching it were not in my plans. They were God's plans for me. I would have missed the opportunity to serve Him if I hadn't been obedient, even though I was nervous.

Understand you may never fully know how God will use your obedience in the lives of others. Be available to be used by the Lord. Know that He equips the called. Step out in courage and embrace new adventures, remain obedient, saying yes to God, and you will grow in faith and trust.

"Jude, a servant of Jesus Christ and a brother of James,
To those who have been called, who are loved in God the Father
and kept for Jesus Christ: Mercy, peace and love be yours in abundance."
~ Jude 1:1-2

78

Mission Day 2020

"For even the Son of Man did not come to be served, but to serve,
and to give his life as a ransom for many."
~ Mark 10:45

"And the King will say, 'I tell you the truth, when you did it to one of
the least of these my brothers and sisters, you were doing it to me!'"
~ Matthew 25:40 (NLT)

The setting for our mission trip to Cozumel, Mexico was at Casa de la Creatividad. This is a creative art center founded in 2017. It is a safe place for neighborhood children to go and learn responsibility and to express themselves through different art media, as well as learn routines and life lessons.

Our assignment was to help at a block party, sponsored by Casa de la Creatividad and the My360 Project. My360Project has a two-fold mission. One is to provide shoes to those in need around the world to help change and save lives. The second is to provide employment and disrupt the cycle of poverty due to lack of education or opportunities. Each shoe is handmade, and My360Project artisans train people from the local communities to make the shoes. The local people are then employed and can provide for their families.

During the party, different art stations were set up for a variety of projects. Each child received a meal and also had the opportunity to decorate their new pair of shoes provided by My360Project.

Christine M. Fisher

Before going to Cozumel, I read John 13:1-20 about Jesus washing the feet of His disciples. We not only washed the children's feet and gave them shoes, but we also served them food and drink. It was symbolic of when Jesus washed His disciple's feet and shared the Last Supper with them.

I was thankful to start with the foot-washing station. The children only spoke Spanish. We were given a cheat sheet with a few phrases like, "Can I wash your feet?" and "Jesus loves you." My cheat sheet disappeared when the wind blew it away. It was hard to understand the children, but they knew what was happening so words weren't necessary.

Though chairs were available for the leaders and children, one volunteer decided to sit on the ground. That seemed more like taking the role of a servant, so I followed his lead. Jesus said,

> "If I then, your Lord and Teacher, have washed your
> feet, you also ought to wash one another's feet."
> ~ John 13:14 (ESV)

As the children came up for their food, I saw the face of Jesus in each one of them. They all had bright, beautiful smiles.

Reflecting on Jesus washing the feet of His disciples showed me four aspects of His character.

The love of Jesus.

"...Having loved his own who were in the world, he loved them to the end."
~ John 13:1

The humility of Jesus.
> He gave us an example of how we need to be humble servants.

The forgiveness of Jesus.
> Jesus knew Judas would betray Him, yet He chose to wash his feet.

The provision for spiritual cleansing.
> The interaction between Jesus and Simon Peter that same night showed how Simon needed not only his feet washed but a spiritual cleansing as well.

I hope and pray the children in Cozumel caught a glimpse of these four things during our time together. Although we didn't speak the same language, I pray our love in action spoke volumes to them.

At the end of our day together, a young girl gave me a hug and smile, which was priceless. I had not washed her feet that day, yet she stole a piece of my heart through her simple act; no words necessary.

It was the perfect ending to a day of serving and sharing Christ with these children in Mexico.

> *"It was just before the Passover Festival. Jesus knew that the hour had come for him to leave this world and go to the Father. Having loved his own who were in the world, he loved them to the end. So he got up from the meal, took off his outer clothing, and wrapped a towel around his waist. After that, he poured water into a basin and began to wash his disciples' feet, drying them with the towel that was wrapped around him."*
> ~ John 13:1, 4-5

79

Welcome Home

When our daughter went to graduate school, she moved four hours away. This was the first time for her to leave home, as she did her undergraduate work locally. She was away for three months before coming home for the Thanksgiving break. We were excited to have her home, and I took the week off work to make the most of every moment. With her home, we enjoyed her favorite restaurants and outings. It was difficult to say good-bye again, but life is continually changing, and things don't stay the same.

Reflecting on welcoming my daughter home reminded me of our relationship with God, giving me a sliver of what He must feel for us, His children.

> Doesn't God long to welcome us home by coming into the right relationship with Him, accepting Him as our Lord and Savior?
> And once we do, doesn't He so patiently wait for us to engage with Him through prayer, reading His love book, the Bible, and through loving others?
> And when we stray from the fold, leaving home to go out on our own, doesn't it break His heart?

As our Father, He too, wants what is best for His children! No matter what we do or where we've been, God's arms are always outstretched to welcome us home. In the story of the prodigal son, this is so evident.

I heard these lines from a song that fit so perfectly.

> "All you need to do is turn around
> And the Father will come running."

Christine M. Fisher

Where are you in your relationship with God? Are you safe at home with Him?

"For this is how God loved the world: He gave his one and only Son, so that everyone who believes in him will not perish but have eternal life."
~ John 3:16 (NLT)

80

Battles

As I watched my son in physical therapy, I thought about all the people who are fighting a personal battle with some ailment, whether physical, emotional, mental, or spiritual. By looking at most of them, you wouldn't know they were fighting a battle. There were people of all ages, from ten to eighty years old, and all walks of life. There were a variety of physical battles fought that day, including a leg, a wrist, an elbow, and in my son's case, a shoulder. One teenage girl caught my eye. Her work ethic was commendable. She put in the hard work to get the victory over her battle. She knew what she needed to do and worked faithfully.

What are the battles you are fighting?

> Are they spiritual or emotional?
> Do you have an eating disorder or lack the discipline to stick with an exercise regimen?
> Perhaps you're trying to be the best at something and can't gain the victory.
> Is it family discord, an illness, or overcoming the death of a loved one?

I'm reminded of the validity of this statement from the book, "The Candymakers" by Wendy Mass. She says, "Be kind, for everyone you meet is fighting a battle you know nothing about."

To fight our battles and win the victory, we need to…

> admit there is a problem.
> show up ready to fight.

Christine M. Fisher

put the work in.

do what we are told when experts help us.

use and avail ourselves to people and "tools."

This slogan, "Your Mountain, Our Journey," is from a place called Peak Performance and hangs on the wall of our physical therapy office. I find comfort in these words as it shows that the staff recognizes their commitment in helping their patients fight their personal physical battles. Along with the slogan are pictures of people who have conquered their physical battles. A few are pictures of athletes who had injuries and went on to play their sport in college and beyond.

For whatever battle you are currently fighting, keep fighting until you are victorious. Put in the work. Remember, you are never alone – God is with you. And share your battle with a trusted friend who will support and encourage you and hold you accountable to help you gain victory.

"Blessed is the one who perseveres under trial because, having stood the test, that person will receive the crown of life that the Lord has promised to those who love him."

~ James 1:12

81

God's Call for You

God calls each of us to different things and He has equipped us with our own unique, spiritual gifts.

There are examples of many people in the Bible who God called:

- ~ Mary - to be the Mother of Jesus, the "tabernacle" for God's only Son.
- ~ John the Baptist - to prepare the way for Jesus to preach repentance.
- ~ Abraham - to be the Father of all nations.
- ~ Samuel - as a youth, to proclaim God's word.
- ~ Moses - to bring God's people out of Egypt.
- ~ Esther - to save God's people, the Jews from annihilation.
- ~ Jeremiah - called as a youth to be a great prophet for God.
- ~ Isaiah - to be a prophet to speak to a corrupt generation.
- ~ The twelve apostles - to heal the sick, preach the good news, and be fishers of men.
- ~ Paul - to preach to the Gentiles.
- ~ Peter - to lead the first church.
- ~ Jesus - to bring salvation to all who believe in Him.

Many times, the people did not feel worthy of their calling.

Moses asked,

> *"Who am I that I should go to Pharaoh and*
> *bring the Israelites out of Egypt?"*
> ~ Exodus 3:11

John the Baptist said,

> *"...But after me comes one who is more powerful*
> *than I, whose sandals I am not fit to carry..."*
> ~ Matthew 3:11

Isaiah said,

> *"'Woe to me!' I cried. 'I am ruined! For I am a man of*
> *unclean lips, and I live among a people of unclean lips, and*
> *my eyes have seen the King, the Lord Almighty.'"*
> ~ Isaiah 6:5

Peter said,

> *"...Go away from me, Lord; I am a sinful man!"*
> ~ Luke 5:8

When God calls you, it involves two major things.

1. Loving the Lord, your God, with all your heart, mind, and soul.

> *"Jesus replied: 'Love the Lord your God with all your heart and with*
> *all your soul and with all your mind. This is the first and greatest*
> *commandment. And the second is like it: Love your neighbor as yourself.'"*
> ~ Matthew 22:37-39

2. Making disciples of all people.

> *"Then Jesus came to them and said,*
> *'...Therefore go and make disciples of all nations,*
> *baptizing them in the name of the Father and of the Son*

and of the Holy Spirit, and teaching them to obey
everything I have commanded you.
And surely I am with you always, to the very end of the age.'"
~ Matthew 28:19-20

God has called and commissioned us. In what ways is God calling you? Living daily for Him and doing "little" things for others are callings from God. We can send cards to the sick, help the poor and broken, pray for others, and speak words of encouragement. Sometimes we need to stretch ourselves and see if there are even bigger things God is calling us to. We might have to put aside our feelings of unworthiness and stop making excuses. We need to remember that when we do what God calls us to, we experience His peace and joy.

God doesn't call the qualified, He qualifies the called! Stay where you are until God calls you into something new. God calls us into things, not just out of them. May you find God's calling in your life, and may you experience His many rewards and blessings.

"You did not choose me, but I chose you and appointed you so that you might
go and bear fruit–fruit that will last – and so that whatever you ask in my
name the Father will give you. This is my command: Love each other."
~ John 15:16-17

82

In the Palms of His Hands

When I am free on the weekends, I continue to help the NICU by holding and loving those little ones who need extra attention. Gazing upon the babies' angelic faces, watching their expressions while holding them in the palms of my hands, is priceless.

So many thoughts run through my head as I hold them. Like, how often we need to rest in the palms of God's hands, taking time to just be with God. It can be through reading His Word, praying, or taking a few moments to be quiet and rest in His presence, in the stillness. Do you take time for these things?

At church, I heard the song *On Eagle's Wings*,[5] written by Michael Joncas. It made me smile and brought tears to my eyes. The refrain says,

> And He will raise you up on eagles' wings
> Bear you on the breath of dawn
> Make you to shine like the sun
> And hold you in the palm of His hand.

It reminds me of this scripture:

> *"See, I have engraved you on the palms of my*
> *hands; your walls are ever before me."*
> ~ Isaiah 49:16

May you pause from the busyness of life and take time to rest in the palms of God's hands. His hands are big enough to hold you. Soak up His love as He gazes upon your face. Remember, He wants only the best for you, His child. Remember His great love for you.

If I am perfectly content sitting and gazing upon a little one in the NICU, how much our heavenly Father must revel in looking at us. We are the perfect creation He formed and planned.

"Everything God does is right—the trademark on all his works is love. God's there, listening for all who pray, for all who pray and mean it. He does what's best for those who fear him—hears them call out and saves them."
~ Psalm 145:17-19 (MSG)

Christine M. Fisher

83

Where Are You?

Jesus says,
"You are so precious to Me. I have given you so much—
the land that you walk on,
the air that you breathe,
all that you have and are.

"But, my friend, where are you?
I need you to be…
My hands,
My feet,
My heart,
each and every day.

"Don't let this world that I've given you
take you away from Me.
I know there are so many 'things'
that pull you in different directions—
away from Me.

"Be concerned with the things that will
last for all eternity, not the temporary
things of this world.

"Make sure you keep Me first in your
life as you go along serving…
your families,
your church community,

your friends,
and everyone you meet.

"I need mostly Your heart
full of love and compassion
to give to others.

"Everyone I place in your path
is an opportunity to share a part of Me."

"Don't just pretend to love others. Really love them. Hate what is wrong.
Hold tightly to what is good."
~ Romans 12:9 (NLT)

84

An Act of Love

One day on my doorstep was a brown bag containing handmade potholders and aprons. The card said, "Just because. Love, Kathy."

Kathy is a friend of the family. Our youngest sons have been friends through the years. One year we set sail on a cruise together. We have good memories of a treasured time spent together, enjoying the sights, food, and company. A few of the aprons had a nautical theme, which was a nice reminder of the cruise.

I messaged Kathy to show my appreciation for her kindness, thanking her for the love she put into making the goodies. Her act of love brought a big smile to my face. Her reply touched me. "The whole time I was making the aprons, I kept thinking of your family helping at the soup kitchen, and I wanted to help the helpers. I wanted you to feel loved and appreciated." I responded, "What an act of love. You are appreciated too." How powerful is that sentiment? She wanted to "help the helpers" and "wanted us to feel loved and appreciated."

With more of God's perfect timing, two days later we received another package. My niece and her husband lovingly made cloth facemasks for our family. They were gifted a sewing machine by a mystery person at the beginning of the pandemic.

An act of love can go a long way to spread kindness and joy to others.

Think of the many acts of love Jesus did. How many times did He lift the spirit of the lowly, the destitute, and the sinner? Didn't He accept them, just as they were, which in turn made them want to change and be better people?

> What acts of love have others given you to make you feel loved and appreciated?
> Can you think of acts of love you've given to make others feel loved and appreciated?

Acts of love make this world a better place.
Yes, we can change the world, one act of love at a time.
Acts of love emit a ripple effect of goodness in this world.
A loving act can go a long way to spread kindness and joy to others.
"Just because" is a great reason to bless another with an act of love.

"Let us think of ways to motivate one another to acts of love and good works."
~ Hebrews 10:24 (NLT)

85

Just One

Dave Pettigrew, an independent Christian musician, was touring with John Waller, who sang, *While I'm Waiting* and *Crazy Faith* featured in the movies *Fireproof* and *War Room*, respectively. Though Dave and John had not met before the tour, they became great friends.

Being independent musicians, their touring responsibilities include driving the van, loading and unloading the equipment, working the merchandise tables, and meeting their fans. Sometimes it entails a lot of work with few attendees.

At the concert I attended, only 25 people were there. I felt sad for Dave and John because of the time and expense of touring. But on days when there were fewer people in attendance, great things still happened. The Lord was at work. They both heard stories of what people were going through and how their ministries offered hope. These musicians also help find sponsors for children in foreign countries to provide education, food, clean water, and healthcare. The concerts with lower attendance garnered more sponsorships for children, changing their lives for the better!

Like Dave and John, I know each day is an opportunity to minister to just one person, without getting distracted by the numbers. As a writer, I am often disappointed to see how few people read my weekly posts. When I started my website, I hoped just one person each week would find a fresh perspective and be drawn closer to God. I need to keep my perspective on the "one," constantly looking for the blessing of each day. God's perfect timing makes me smile.

One day as I took a walk, I passed one of my neighbors. I knew she was grieving the anniversary of her mother's death. She told me about her rough day as we greeted each other. She is the principal at a nearby school, and I could sense her relief that the workday was over. As we conversed, a neighborhood boy came over to talk with her. He expressed his appreciation for the good foundation he received at her school. I hope our conversations were an encouragement to her, knowing someone cared. Just one interaction can change someone's life for the better!

When pondering the thought of "just one," I remembered the Bible story of the lost sheep.

> *"What do you think? If a man owns a hundred sheep, and one*
> *of them wanders away, will he not leave the ninety-nine on*
> *the hills and go to look for the one that wandered off?*
> *And if he finds it, truly I tell you, he is happier about that one*
> *sheep than about the ninety-nine that did not wander off."*
> ~ Matthew 18:12-13

This parable lets us know how Jesus, indeed, cares about "just one." He will pursue that one, which shows us the importance of "just one" life. And if you were the only person God created, you would be His "just one." He would have sent Jesus, His only Son, to die for you. You are that special to God!

Keep making a difference, day by day, in the life of "just one."

> *"God showed how much he loved us by sending his one and only Son*
> *into the world so that we might have eternal life through him."*
> ~ 1 John 4:9 (NLT)

86

Moving In

One day while volunteering at the NICU, a newborn boy was brought in. He was in an isolette, fighting for his life. As his parents came in to see their little one, the mom coming over from the maternity ward, I thought about the brokenness they were experiencing. A few weeks later, the little boy was strong enough to be moved to an infant bassinet.

Since seeing him the first time, I had been praying for him because he was so small and angelic. My love for snuggling babies gave me the desire to hold him and pray over him. Much to my surprise, one day a nurse gave me permission to hold him, explaining he had a procedure that day and could use the extra touch.

It was both an honor and blessing to hold this little boy, still tiny though he was 20 days old. I knew I was holding another miracle, even though we are all miracles of life. The next day, as I sat in the same spot, the parents of the infant came in to take him home. I try not to make eye contact with the parents because I don't want to invade their privacy. I could hear the dad read what was written on the shirt they brought for him to wear home. It said, "Peace out, NICU, I'm moving in with my parents."

As I rocked a sleeping baby in my arms, I couldn't help but think about the parallel with the glorious day God calls us home to spend eternity with Him. What joy that day will hold for us, just as it did for the parents of that baby boy who waited 20 days to take their son home.

May we, with joy, say, "Peace out, world. I'm moving in with my Dad!" What a glorious homecoming that will be!

When we will finally get to see God face-to-face,
glorifying Him even more than on this earth,
where there is only light,
we will be safe in His embrace!

"Do not love the world or the things in the world. If anyone loves the world, the love of the Father is not in him. For all that is in the world– the desires of the flesh and the desires of the eyes and pride of life–is not from the Father but is from the world. And the world is passing away along with its desires, but whoever does the will of God abides forever."
~ 1 John 2:15-17 (ESV)

87

Listen

We believe and know in our heart God is always there, ready to listen, both in our joys and sorrows. After all, He is Abba, our Father, who loves us more than anyone in the world. He is our Creator and knew us before the world existed. It's also nice to have a human who listens to us. God provides people to support us, pray for and with us, and share in our time of need. It's important to keep our eyes and heart open to recognize these people.

Do you often feel like you and God can solve all your problems yourself? Maybe you feel that you don't need a "human" to share with. Perhaps this is because you have been hurt by someone not holding your words in confidence, or you fear being misunderstood. Maybe it's difficult to be vulnerable with someone because you don't want to be wounded.

God does not want us isolated from each other and afraid to share with others. Shouldn't we live like the saying, "No man is an island?" We need others, and we need to extend ourselves to others.

One blessing we tend to underuse is the gift of listening.

I received a text from a friend asking if I was available to meet. She wanted to share the stressful events of her week. I was both grateful and humbled this friend wanted to share with me. I tried to be present and listen by having empathy for what she was going through. The best thing I could do was pray with her and the situation. When I left, my friend was a little more peaceful.

Take the time to listen to people, especially in their times of trials and tribulations. Be Christ to them.

Listen...

> without feeling the need to offer solutions to what they are going through.
> focusing your attention on the person sharing.
> trying to understand the emotions of their experience.
> not judging or condemning them.
> letting them share.

It is also vital we take time to listen to God. He reminds us daily how much He loves us and how He is continually working in our lives. We are filled with His love, peace, and joy when we listen to Him.

Sometimes we may hear the audible voice of God in a decision we are trying to make, but more often, we hear Him speak through...

> His beautiful creation.
> the silence of the night.
> something someone shares with us.
> inspiring music.
> God orchestrated moments.
> His Word.

> "Be a good listener. Your ears will never get you in trouble." –Frank Tyger

> *"And I have other sheep that are not of this fold. I must bring them also, and they will listen to my voice. So there will be one flock, one shepherd. For this reason the Father loves me, because I lay down my life that I may take it up again."*
> ~ John 10:16-17 (ESV)

Christine M. Fisher

88

Take My Yoke

"Then Jesus said, 'Come to me, all of you who
are weary and carry heavy burdens,
and I will give you rest. Take my yoke upon you. Let me teach you,
because I am humble and gentle at heart, and
you will find rest for your souls.
For my yoke is easy to bear, and the burden I give you is light.'"
~ Matthew 11:28-30 (NLT)

A yoke is a type of harness that connects a pair of oxen. What does it mean to be yoked to Jesus? We come together with Jesus. He leads and we follow. He shares our burdens.

If we visualize Jesus coming alongside us with His yoke, we realize that Jesus is calling us to connect with Him. His yoke fits perfectly and is lighter than the one we try to carry by ourselves.

Jesus says ...

> *"Be with me."* He is also calling us to go with Him in the same direction, as He guides us. We cannot wander off.
> *"Follow me."* As we cooperate with Him, we have no choice but to follow Him and keep His pace.
> *"Work with me."* We are joined in kingdom work, realizing everything we do has an eternal impact.

In 1989, William and Caroline Bandera wanted to do something for the community to let them know people cared. They provided a free, hot Christmas meal that year and served 69 people. Thirty-one years later, relatives and volunteers prepped and served close to 3,000 dinners! Volunteers delivered 1,600 meals to the homebound. The remaining meals were take-out at four different locations in the area due to the pandemic.

Finding out this event needed help was a ripple effect of my sending a text to a friend to share a God moment with her. She casually mentioned a few ways she was spreading holiday cheer with some ministries, which piqued my interest. Little did I know God would use that simple text to give me the honor of being able to serve three days with this event.

I did not know the prep work for the Christmas dinner began in early December. The event was well organized, from the beginning to the end. Every day there was a list of duties, each one explained, with specific times, number of people needed, and volunteer spots available. What are the chances my friend and I would be serving on the same day, at the same time, sitting next to each other, carving turkeys? God is good.

My youngest son, home from college for a few weeks, was willing to serve for two days. His youth and muscles came in handy for heavy lifting. On Christmas Day, my husband, son, and I assembled the to-go containers at a new site. Two volunteers needed help prepping the mashed potatoes. I was in awe to learn their shift started at 3 a.m. By the time we arrived at 9:30 a.m., they had already cut, cooked, and mashed eleven 50 lb. bags of potatoes. There were still four bags left. My son helped carry the pots of potatoes to get them ready for the distribution locations. My husband and I cut the rest of the potatoes. The cooking and cleaning up process of took three men until after 1 p.m.

The scripture from Matthew 11:28-30 came to mind as I thought about the work that went into preparing for the dinner. There were 125 volunteers yoked together to make this event happen. Each person was important to make it successful. One by one, coming together to serve in His name made the burden bearable. One person would not be able to do it. When

Christine M. Fisher

someone was tired and weary, another person came along to assist. The burden was made lighter with many people and hands wanting to serve others, to share with those in need. The organizer of the event said, "The honor is having so many people willing to be servants when the times are and have been so troubled."

Jesus continually desires to be yoked with us. Do we desire to be yoked with Him? Jesus takes charge of the yoke and gently guides us. We can trust Him through everything, and together, we can be confident our burdens are lighter.

With Jesus leading, we…

> know we are going in the right direction.
> will stay on the path and not wander.
> will not shoulder the burden alone.
> have more strength.
> are not alone.
> are supported and loved.

> *"I hate those who cling to worthless idols; as for me, I trust in the Lord. I will be glad and rejoice in your love, for you saw my affliction and knew the anguish of my soul. You have not given me into the hands of the enemy but have set my feet in a spacious place."*
> ~ Psalm 31:6-8

89

Your Story

Your life is a story that only you can write to our Creator, God Almighty. No two people have the same story; each story is unique. There are circumstances in your life you can control and those you cannot. Every day brings many decisions. You make choices that shape and mold your life's story, which contains many chapters. It can be based on the stages of life–infancy, childhood, teenager, young adult, adult, elderly person. The chapters can also represent significant events in your life.

When you are an infant, you depend solely on your caregiver to meet your needs. As you grow, you have some control over your gift to God. As a teenager, you have even more options in deciding how your story will be written.

> Will you stand up for your beliefs, or will you follow the crowd and compromise your faith?

When you are a young adult, you have more freedom and even greater control over writing your story to God. The opportunities are endless. As an adult, you have the most potential for writing your story to God. You are now on your own, responsible for yourself.

> How you react to the various situations in life is a big part of your story.

> Have you viewed your life in this way?
> Do the things you busy yourself with reflect that view?
> How about the decisions you make, the places you go, and the people in your life?

With God's help, you have the power and freedom to write your personal story, your gift to Him. It is never too late to begin anew if your story is not what you want it to be. If there is a chapter in your life you don't like, you can seek God's forgiveness and move on to bigger and better things.

God is always there, waiting for us and waiting to guide us. Wouldn't it be great to look back and say you are satisfied with your story? Your story is your gift to God! Every life is truly a special gift from God. What you do with it and how you live it is your gift to God.

"As the Father has loved me, so have I loved you. Now remain in my love."
~ John 15:9

90

Perfection

One day while serving in the NICU, I held a wee one with the reputation of being a screamer. He was in the unfortunate circumstance of being an opiate baby. These babies get off to a rougher start in life and tend to have tremors, are more irritable, and have sleep problems. He fussed when I first picked him up and struggled to take the pacifier. I softly sang to him as we rocked. As he lay peacefully in my arms, I thought about the problems and issues he faced, and was overwhelmed with the thought and word, perfection.

God looks at this little guy as perfection. Despite all his issues, God's perception of him does not change. God looks at and sees only perfection.

When God looks at us, He sees perfection! Yes, even you, the one reading these words. You are perfection to God! I bet you are thinking, "What? That can't be right!"

> Yes, you are far from perfect, and you don't always make the right choices.
> Yes, you may have physical imperfections.
> Yes, you may sin daily, despite trying not to.
> Yes, you may have emotional scars from some of the bad things you have experienced.
> Yes, you may even get mad and scream at God for the "bad" things you are experiencing.
> Yes, you may even have an addiction of some sort.

> You may ask, "How can I be perfection to God?"

Christine M. Fisher

YOU ARE MADE IN HIS IMAGE!

"This is the book of the generations of Adam.
When God created man, he made him in the likeness of God."
~ Genesis 5:1 (ESV)

YOU ARE GOD'S SON OR DAUGHTER!

"For in Christ Jesus you are all sons (daughters) of God, through faith."
~ Galatians 3:26 (ESV)

YOU HAVE BEEN CHOSEN BY GOD!

"Even before he made the world, God loved us and chose us in
Christ to be holy and without fault in his eyes."
~ Ephesians 1:4 (NLT)

YOU ARE LOVED UNCONDITIONALLY BY GOD!

"But God showed his great love for us by sending Christ
to die for us while we were still sinners."
~ Romans 5:8 (NLT)

YOU ARE MADE PURE, HOLY, AND FREE FROM SIN
BECAUSE GOD SENT JESUS TO DIE FOR YOU!

"God has united you with Christ Jesus. For our benefit God
made him to be wisdom itself. Christ made us right with God;
he made us pure and holy, and he freed us from sin."
~ 1 Corinthians 1:30 (NLT)

May you understand and experience the great love God, our Father, has
for you, His own child, the one He created. Even when you are sleeping

soundly tonight, God is looking down on you, His child, with love and peace, seeing perfection.

Look at your reflection in a mirror and say, "Perfection!" Yes, that is what God sees too! God sees perfection!

"By this is love perfected with us, so that we may have confidence for the day of judgment, because as he is so also are we in this world. There is no fear in love, but perfect love casts out fear. For fear has to do with punishment, and whoever fears has not been perfected in love."
~ 1 John 4:17-18 (ESV)

Christine M. Fisher

CONCLUSION

I think it perfect to close the devotional by sharing this prayer and blessing on the following page. We are given one life, a short span of years to embrace God and His great love for us while on this earth. Our challenge is then to live out that love and share it with others. May this be your daily prayer as you seek to glorify our Father by your life.

Radiate, shine, and illuminate Jesus' fragrance, light, and love into the lives of all you encounter as He continually fills your heart with His love.

Radiating Christ Prayer

Dear Jesus,
Help me to spread Your fragrance wherever I go.
Flood my soul with Your spirit and Your life.
Penetrate and possess my whole being so utterly,
that my life may only be a radiance of Yours.

Shine through me, and be so in me
that every soul I come in contact with
may feel Your presence in my soul.
Let them look up and see no longer me, but only Jesus!

Stay with me and then I shall begin to shine as You shine,
so to shine as to be a light to others.
The light, O Jesus, will be all from You; none of it will be mine.
It will be you, shining on others through me.

Let me thus praise You the way You love best,
by shining on those around me.
Let me preach You without preaching, not by words but by my example,
by the catching force of the sympathetic influence of what I do,
the evident fullness of the love my heart bears to You. Amen.

–Cardinal John Henry Newman

ABOUT THE AUTHOR

Christine Fisher defines herself in this way, "I am a simple, ordinary gal, a child of God, a lover of Jesus, a daughter, wife and mother. I am also an introvert who enjoys sharing God-stories through writing and in small intimate settings."

Christine models her life after the ministry of Jesus. She serves others in little things, like Christmas caroling to shut-ins, holding the tiniest of babies in the NICU, giving rides to those without transportation, serving in the soup kitchen, holding the hands of friends, and praying over strangers. She finds joy in being an encourager by sending cards, praying, visiting, and providing affirming words.

Through the written word, Christine shares what is in her heart about Jesus, hoping to inspire and encourage others in their faith journey. She has the "eyes of God" and sees His presence, goodness, and grace through the ordinary things in life, whether it be a seashell on the beach or a boulder on the mountaintop. Being able to express her thoughts in writing and through the spoken word has helped her deepen her faith and grow closer in her relationship with Jesus.

Christine and her husband, Mark, live in upstate New York. They are the parents of three adult children. She enjoys spending quiet time in nature worshiping the Creator.

"Publish his glorious deeds among the nations.
Tell everyone about the amazing things he does."
~ 1 Chronicles 16:24 (NLT)

"I am the vine; you are the branches. If you remain in me and I in you, you will bear much fruit; apart from me you can do nothing!"
~ John 15:5

"For great is your love, higher than the heavens; your faithfulness reaches to the skies. Be exalted, O God, above the heavens; let your glory be over all the earth."
~ Psalm 108:4-5

"As the rain and the snow come down from heaven, and do not return to it without watering the earth and making it bud and flourish, so that it yields seed for the sower and bread for the eater, so is my word that goes out from my mouth: It will not return to me empty but will accomplish what I desire and achieve the purpose for which I sent it. You will go out in joy and be led forth in peace..."
~ Isaiah 55:10-12

You can receive Christine's weekly posts by subscribing at: www.hopetoinspireyou.com or by following her on Facebook at *hopetoinspireyou.*

Other books by Christine:
God's Presence Illuminated: Treasured Thoughts to Inspire Hope and Light

NOTES

Day 18 | Family
[1] https://www.mhskids.org/student-tatiana/true-meaning-family

Day 35 | Cascading Love
[2] *Offering.* Words and Music by Mac Powell, Mark Lee, Brad Avery, Tai Anderson and David Carr. © 2003 Consuming Fire Music. Administered by EMI Christian Music Publishing. All rights reserved.

Day 67 | You've Got a Friend
[3] *You've Got a Friend.* Words and Music by Carole King. © 1971 Colgems-EMI Music, Inc. Administered by Sony/ATV Music Publishing LLC, Nashville, TN. All rights reserved.

Day 71 | Blinded
[4] *Greater Than You Know.* Words and Music by Weston Skaggs. © 2020 Weston Skaggs and Old Bear Records. All rights reserved.

Day 82 | In the Palms of His Hands
[5] *On Eagle's Wings.* Words and Music by Michael Joncas. © 1979 Jan Michael Joncas. Published by OCP, Portland, OR. All rights reserved.

Made in the USA
Middletown, DE
02 March 2022

62014707R00150